DEMOCRATIC LEGISLATIVE INSTITUTIONS

■ Comparative Politics Series

Gregory S. Mahler, Editor

POWER AND RITUAL IN THE ISRAEL LABOR PARTY
A Study in Political Anthropology
Myron J. Aronoff

COMPARATIVE POLITICAL SYSTEMS
Policy Performance and Social Change
Charles F. Andrain

DEMOCRATIC LEGISLATIVE INSTITUTIONS
A Comparative View
David M. Olson

BLAMING THE GOVERNMENT
Citizens and the Economy in Five European Democracies
Christopher Anderson

POLITICAL CULTURE AND CONSTITUTIONALISM
A Comparative Approach
Edited by Daniel P. Franklin and Michael Baun

COMPARATIVE
POLITICS
SERIES

DEMOCRATIC LEGISLATIVE INSTITUTIONS

A Comparative View

DAVID M. OLSON

M.E. Sharpe
Armonk, New York
London, England

Library of Congress Cataloging-in-Publication Data

Olson, David M.
Democratic legislative institutions : a comparative view / David M. Olson.
p.   cm. — (Comparative politics)
Includes bibliographical references (p.   ) and index.
ISBN 1-56324-314-8. — ISBN 1-56324-315-6 (pbk.)
1. Legislative bodies.
2. Democracy.
3. Comparative government.
I. Title.
II. Series: Comparative politics (Armonk, N.Y.)
JF501.047   1994
321.8—dc20
94-18913
CIP

Printed in the United States of America

The paper used in this publication meets the minimum requirements of
American National Standard for Information Sciences—
Permanence of Paper for Printed Library Materials,
ANSI Z 39.48-1984.

MV (c)	10	9	8	7	6	5	4	3	2	1
MV (p)	10	9	8	7	6	5	4	3	2	1

This book is dedicated to

Amy and Eric,

who in their very different ways
provided a happy environment
in which to work.

Contents

List of Boxes, Tables, and Figures   xi

Preface   xiii

Acknowledgments   xv

Chapter 1. Legislatures in Today's Democracies   1
Attributes of Legislatures   3
Legislatures and Policy Decisions   9

Chapter 2. The Members: Representatives and Legislators   13
The Job: Dimensions of Time   13
The Job: Activities and Roles   16
Experience and Characteristics of Members   20
The Members and the Institution   27

Chapter 3. Political Parties:
The Internal Organization of Parliament, I   31
Parties and Committees Compared   31
Party Systems   32
The Ideological Spectrum   37
Organization of the Chamber   39
Party Officers   43
Party Voting   50
External Links   53
Summary   54

Chapter 4. Committees:
The Internal Organization of Parliament, II   56
Types of Committees   56
Activities and Tasks   59
Members and Officers   64
Committees, Parties, and Legislation on the Floor   66
Committee Documents   67
Coordination   70
The New and the Old   71
Summary   72

Chapter 5. Legislative–Executive Relations   74
Constitutional Design and Chief Executives   74
Party System and Government Selection   79
Selection of Candidates for Chief Executive   82
Working Relationships: Legislation   83
Additional Working Relationships   89
A Troubled Relationship   92

Chapter 6. The Electorate and the Public:
Elections and Interest Groups   94
Electoral and District Systems   94
Electoral Campaigns and Political Parties   99
Voter Response   103
Districting and Campaign Finance   106
Interest Groups   108
Election System Controversies   111
Summary   114

Chapter 7. Parliaments at the Beginning   115
New Institution, New Members, New Tasks   116
The Members   117
Rules and Procedures   119
Internal Organization I: Political Parties   121
Internal Organization II: Committees   124
Staff Support   125
Relationships with the Executive   126
The Constitution   126
The Public and Mass Media   127

The Former USSR   128
Summary   130

Chapter 8. Legislatures in the Policy Process   132
External Environment   133
Internal Characteristics   137
Policy Attributes   142

Appendix A: Stages of Legislative Procedure   145

**Appendix B: The Vocabulary of Parliaments
and Legislatures**   153

**Appendix C: Congress and Parliament:
American and British English**   159

References   161

Author Index   173

Subject Index   176

About the Author   184

List of Boxes, Tables, and Figures

Boxes

1.1 Parliaments, Laws, and Kings: The Glorious Revolution   2
1.2 Order in the House   9
2.1 What Profession Is This?   14
2.2 Privacy?   15
2.3 Whose Experience?   17
2.4 The House of Lords   26
2.5 Who Is a Revolutionary?   28
2.6 The Virtuous Spiral   29
3.1 Churchill on the Shape of the Party System   41
3.2 The Speaker Speaks   42
3.3 Perils of the Minority   45
3.4 The Rapture of Party   48
4.1 Talk and Work in Parliaments   57
4.2 British Departmental Committees and Administration: Two-Way Interaction   61
4.3 British Trade and Industry Committee Press Notice   62
4.4 Committee Documents by Country and Type   69
5.1 With Friends Like These . . . ?   78
5.2 Who Worries? From the Prime Minister to the President   79
5.3 Japan's Liberal Democratic Party Factionalism   81
5.4 Government and Legislation   90
6.1 Matthew Effect   99
6.2 The Public as Target: Lobbying and President Clinton's Health Care Proposals   111

6.3 A British Group on Lobbying   112
7.1 Authoritarian System Transformation: Readings   116
7.2 The Collapse of Communist Rule in
     Central Europe: Readings   118

Tables

1.1 Models of Democratic Legislatures   11
2.1 Occupations of Legislators   22
3.1 Two-Party Systems in Britain, the United States,
     and Canada: Seats in the Legislature   34
3.2 Multiparty Systems: Seats in Parliament   35
4.1 Contrasting U.S. and British Committee Systems   58
5.1 Bills in the German Bundestag, by Source   84
6.1 British Parliamentary Election: Votes and Seats 1992   97
6.2 Canadian Parliamentary Elections:
     Votes and Seats 1988, 1993   98
6.3 Swedish Parliamentary Election: Votes and Seats 1991   100
6.4 Spanish Parliamentary Elections:
     Votes and Seats 1989, 1993   104
6.5 Election System Controversies   113
8.1 Factors and Indicators in the Policy
     Participation of Parliaments   133
A.1 Steps in Legislative Procedure in Selected Legislatures   146

Figures

3.1 Floor Plan of British House of Commons   40
5.1 Parliamentary and Presidential-Congressional Systems   75

Preface

This book was initially drafted in Prague for students at Charles University only two years after the collapse of communism. It will, I hope, also be useful for students in established, as well as beginning, democracies.

Democratic legislative bodies are continually changing. Not only do we increase our knowledge of existing and stable democratic legislatures, but the recent transformations of authoritarian systems in Latin America and Southern Europe, and now in Central Europe, the republics of the former Soviet Union, and in Africa, have created entirely new legislatures.

New members of new legislatures in newly formed democratic political systems have a unique opportunity—at times it may seem a burden—to experiment and to develop new ways of organizing and acting. They are not condemned to repeat either the mistakes or the successes of the existing democracies.

The information I have learned about the new legislatures of both Central Europe and Africa is included in this book. I have visited and researched parliaments in Poland and the former Federal Assembly of the Czech and Slovak Federal Republic, and in Nigeria and other African countries. There are now, in the 1990s, many legislatures at the beginning of their development. Special attention—mostly in the form of speculation because we have little research—is given to beginning legislatures in chapter 7.

The chapters of this book may be read in any order convenient to the reader. The three appendices contain reference sources that may be consulted throughout the reading of the book.

Self-government is an adventure, and legislatures are one expression of that adventure. Research, likewise, is an adventure, an exploration of the unknown. This book is an invitation not only to learn what is currently known but also to expand the frontiers of knowledge by undertaking new research.

David M. Olson
Prague, Czech Republic
February 1992
and
Greensboro, North Carolina
April 1994

Acknowledgments

I have personally visited most of the parliaments described in any detail in this book. I am greatly indebted to the many members, staff, reporters, and academic researchers for their extraordinary willingness and ability to share their knowledge and insights about their parliaments with a roving visitor. They have put up with me more than once, for I have been in their countries several times, and some have been able to visit my university as well.

I have relied upon numerous persons in each country. I list only one per country to indicate, through them, my gratitude to the many others who have given of their time and energies to help me understand their parliaments, their politics, and their countries. They have all conspired to make me both better fed and less ignorant than when I arrived: Michael Ryle, United Kingdom; Oyeleye Oyediran, Nigeria; Magnus Isberg, Sweden; Stanislaw Gebethner, Poland; Jana Reschova, Czech Republic; Danica Sivakova, Slovakia; and C.E.S. Franks, Canada.

The intellectual perspective of this book is most clearly summarized in the last chapter. That chapter, in turn, rests upon a long series of conferences organized through and partially funded by several organizations, none of which should be held responsible for the contents of this book: the Legislative Specialists Research Committee of the International Political Science Association, the National Endowment for the Humanities, Duke University, the North American Federalism Project at the University of California, Berkeley, and the Graduate Research Council of the University of North Carolina at Greensboro. Research in specific countries has been supported by grants from the Canadian Embassy, the Swedish Bicentennial Fund, International Research and Exchanges Board, and the Fulbright program.

In addition, I have had the happy experience of visiting at several universities in Europe, and of lecturing to student and governmental audiences in Europe, both East and West, and in Africa. I was fortunate to spend a whole semester at Charles University, Prague, on a Fulbright grant. To all the many people in these institutions, I extend my appreciation for their ability to ask probing questions about my ideas and their willingness to explain their ideas to me.

The manuscript leading to this book has been reviewed, at various stages, by students at Rice University and the University of Mississippi, and by my own students. Their comments and suggestions have been both entertaining and useful. I appreciate the cooperation of Professors Keith Hamm and Gregory Mahler at their respective universities. Professor David Wood of the University of Missouri reviewed the whole manuscript, rescuing me from errors of both commission and omission. At my university, colleagues in both political science and history have assisted at all stages of my thinking; particularly helpful have been Christian Schafmeister, as my German reviewer, and Gregory Ferguson, as my research assistant.

I would welcome communications from readers both to rectify my errors and to add to my knowledge about legislative institutions in democratic political systems, both new and old.

Legislatures in
Today's Democracies

What's Parliament?
Parliament is half way between a museum and a theater.
(Street joke, Prague, 1992)

Parliaments—or legislatures—are the keystone of a democratic political system; they are also the most fragile component of any state. Law of the highest order, save for constitutional law, emanates from the legislature. But at the same time, legislatures are the most vulnerable to dismissal by military coup or party *diktat*.

In democratic systems, of all governmental institutions, legislatures are the most accessible to the public. The executive is advised in private, and disputes and alternatives are developed behind the executive office's closed doors. The judiciary also makes its decisions in secret. It is only the legislature whose arguments and disagreements are displayed in public. If it deliberates in secret, it can be criticized, but if it debates in public, it can be ridiculed.

Legislatures, or parliaments, are also paradoxical and even contradictory institutions, for they join society to the legal structure of authority in the state. On one hand, legislatures are representative bodies: they reflect the sentiments and opinions of the citizens. On the other hand, legislatures are the source of law by which the country is governed: they literally "legislate." The union of both traits in one body is the source of their unique importance in democratic political systems, as illustrated by the theoretical claims of John Locke and the assertion of power by Parliament during England's "Glorious Revolution" (see Box 1.1).

Box 1.1

Parliaments, Laws, and Kings: The Glorious Revolution

From John Locke:

"The first and fundamental positive Law of all Commonwealths, is the establishing of the Legislative Power . . . ; [N]or can any Edict of any Body else . . . have the force and obligation of a Law, which has not its Sanction from that Legislative, which the publick has chosen and appointed."

Second Treatise, ch. XI (1689)
(Quoted in Kurland and Lerner 1987, 615–16)

From the English Bill of Rights:

"The pretended power of dispensing with laws or the execution of laws by regal authority, as it hath been assumed and exercised of late, is illegal . . . levying money for or to the use of the Crown by pretense of prerogative without grant of Parliaments . . . is illegal . . . [A]nd that for redress of all grievances and for the amending, strengthening and preserving of the laws Parliaments ought to be held frequently."

1689
(Quoted in Bailey 1971, 15)

Legislatures meet in large, often ornate palaces, they observe elaborate rules and procedures, and in their solemn and stately dignity, they express the grandeur of the state and the serious purpose of defining and enacting the law. This grand and stately character of legislatures, however, can be contradicted by unseemly arguments, by partisan strife, and by at least the appearance of an inability to arrive at any kind of decision at all.

There are many interchangeable nouns for parliaments and legislatures. In the English language at least, there is no single term that encompasses both these words. The word "parliament" comes from the British Parliament, and is often used in conjunction with the broader designation of a "parliamentary system" of government. The U.S. Congress cannot properly be called a "parliament" in the British sense, for it neither selects nor unseats the chief executive (Bagehot 1963, 220). While the term "legislature" is suitable to the U.S. Congress, some would argue that the same term is not appropriate for the British Parliament (Steffani 1990, 273–74).

Other words are sometimes used: congress, assembly, general court. There are also many specific designations in each language: Riksdagen and Stortinget in the Scandinavian languages, Bundestag and Reichstag in German, Cortes and Congresso in Spanish, and Sejm in Polish, for example. An English-language word often used to designate the parliaments of continental Europe and of Japan is "Diet." This book uses both terms, "parliament" and "legislature," interchangeably as generic terms for the elected representative body.

This book examines parliaments or legislatures in their many dimensions. This first chapter reviews the distinctive attributes of legislatures compared with the other entities of government, and considers the legislature within its wider political environment. The human beings who become legislators, or "Members of Parliament," are discussed in chapter 2. We also consider the internal structure of parliaments, beginning with political parties in chapter 3, and turn in chapter 4 turn to committees, the workshops of legislative activity.

We then examine legislatures in relationship to their major external partners, the executive in chapter 5, and the public in chapter 6. In the final two chapters, we consider the unique problems and opportunities confronting a new parliament at the beginning of a new political system, and conclude with a review of the components of an active legislature within a democratic political system.

Attributes of Legislatures

Legislatures differ from the other organs of government in several critical respects. First, they differ in how they are constituted: they are the primary representative institution within a democratic society. Second, they differ in their functions: they may be the primary means within a democracy for the definition and enactment of law and public policy. Third, if legislatures are vital and active, they will also differ from other institutions of government in their organizational and procedural characteristics.

Constitutive Attributes

Legislative bodies differ in their composition from other governmental entities in several essential respects. They are, first, the primary representative institution within the governmental structure. They are, second, the only institution of government with many members, all of whom are usually selected on a geographic basis. They are, third, elected. They are, fourth, comprised of many members who are formal equals of each other. All of these attributes concern the composition and membership of legislatures.

Representativeness

Legislatures slowly evolved as a means of representing society in councils with royal authority. Representation is a complex, even an elusive concept (Pitkin 1967). One component of that term, however, was uppermost in royal minds in summoning the parliament: as a representative body, it had the power to convey consent of the population to royal requests (sometimes demands) for increased taxes. In turn, the monarch had to listen to "grievances," the representatives' complaints about appointed officials and their administration of royal affairs (Marongiu 1968). Those grievances were often expressed through petitions, leading to both judicial decisions in specific instances and legislation expressing more general principles (Carroll and Smith 1991, 695–96; Williamson 1931, 118).

Simply to exist as a representative body was the legislature's original purpose and, for a long time, this was its only function. The other functions of law and policy have been added slowly and, in many societies, uncertainly.

Geographic and Numerous

As representative bodies, a parliament's members both are numerous and are usually selected from geographic areas. No one person could "represent" the whole society. A large body with members coming from different geographic regions of the country has a better chance of "representation" than does even a large group consisting of only the king's friends at court. A geographic and thus dispersed and varied base was an essential ingredient of representation. Early English parliaments consisted of two knights from each shire (or county), so that parliaments contained many members from the whole geographic reach of the king's realm (Loewenberg and Patterson 1979, 45–47).

Elective

Elections are complicated means of achieving what appears to be a simple objective—the selection of representatives. How shall the knights from each shire be selected?

If there are even more than two eligible persons to make the choice of an official, then a rudimentary election procedure can evolve. For generations before anyone even thought of "democracy" in Western Europe, popes were (as they are now) selected by the College of Cardinals through an internal voting procedure. Emperors of the Holy Roman Empire were similarly selected, as were medieval kings of Poland. Elections to the early parliaments were not very different, in that a very small number of persons were eligible to vote for their representatives.

A crucial innovation from the United States, by about 1820, was the elimination of property as a prerequisite to the right to vote. That is, the few became the many. For the first time, ordinary persons, the masses as opposed to the elites, the poor as opposed to the rich, could vote for representatives in Congress as well as for presidential candidates. Only later were racial and gender restrictions eliminated in the United States, and gender and religious restrictions eliminated in democratic Europe.

Equality

There is only one president or prime minister, and each administrative department has only one minister at a time. But a legislature is a plural body. The equally elected and equally representative members are each other's formal equals. As a result of these constitutive attributes, the decision-making procedures of the U.S. Congress have developed as collective procedures. The elaborate decisional procedures within the White House or British Cabinet are designed to develop and channel advice for the chief executive's personal decision. The elaborate decisional procedures within legislatures are designed to develop, by contrast, a collective agreement. That collective judgment is best symbolized by roll call votes, in which each member has one vote just like every other member. The elaborate internal organization and procedures of legislatures are based upon the equality of the many representatives. While there may be a "prime minister," there is no "prime legislator."

These four constitutive attributes together define the major characteristics of a legislative assembly and together differentiate its membership and composition from other governmental institutions in democratic political systems. The executive is now either directly or indirectly elective, and thus can also claim to be representative. The judiciary is often a plural body—with nine members on the U.S. Supreme Court, for example—and thus makes decisions by voting, and the justices even issue dissenting opinions. It is only the legislative body, however, that possesses all four of these attributes together, and possesses each one of them to a considerable degree.

Functions in the Governmental System

Several broad purposes of legislatures flow from these four constitutive attributes, and further differentiate them from other governmental institutions: policy, law, interaction with the chief executive, and development of public attitudes. Several additional tasks, which vary among countries, can also be assigned to legislatures.

Policy

While the legislature is certainly not the only source of decisions about government policy within a political system—the executive branch is the most common other source—the legislature *is* the most authoritative.

A legislature's function to decide government policy stems from the historic "power of the purse" of the English Parliament discussed above as the basis for its representative character. With the advent of the modern state to cope with the consequences of industrialization, the work load of government increased immeasurably. Only for the past 100 years have any governments been sufficiently complicated and busy to require the full-time service of a legislature, and for any legislature to need the professional services of an expert staff. The policy function is the legislature's most recently acquired function.

Law

Legislatures historically are the authoritative source of statutory law. Statutory law, subordinate to constitutions, is superior to all other forms of law, including administrative regulations. Some, but certainly not all, policy statements by legislatures are enacted in the form of statutes. In stable democracies, the policy function of legislatures, even if expressed through statutes, has become more important in the modern era than has the legal formulation of its actions (Blondel 1973, 16–20).

Chief Executive

Legislatures interact with chief executives and with administrative agencies in a variety of ways. In parliamentary systems, the parliament selects the prime minister. The institution that selects can then also deselect. Although this specific activity is denied to a congress within a separation-of-powers system, the separate and independent congress has the potential to speak and act more independently of the executive than do parliaments within parliamentary systems (King 1976).

Public Attitudes

Finally, all legislatures participate in the formation of public attitudes toward the whole political system. As representative and decisional bodies, they have an opportunity to help knit the diversity of the state's population into a cohesive whole. This potentially supportive relationship has a two-way dynamic: the legislature makes authoritative decisions that are binding upon the population, and the legislature, if it can limit the executive, can also convey public consent to the resulting policies of the state (Mezey 1979, 7–13).

Procedural Attributes

Both as a representative and as a legally powerful body in the development of public policies, a legislature is encouraged to develop careful procedural rules. As a body of many equal members, a legislature also develops elaborate internal organization. Legislatures' unique characteristics also lead to careful and fair procedures: legislatures express conflict, they express partisanship, and they do so in public view (Loewenberg and Patterson 1979, 23–24).

Conflict

Legislatures institutionalize conflict. As representative institutions, they are designed to encompass the diversity of their societies. They are intended to mirror the whole society. If there are wide societal agreements, legislatures reflect them. But more commonly, there are deep-seated disagreements. The purpose of a legislature, more than of other governmental entities, is to reflect and express those disagreements. Conflict expression is an essential part of "representation." It is because legislatures express conflicts that it is essential that all members be equal; otherwise, some points of view would be more equal than others.

Partisanship

As elected bodies, legislatures include members of many political parties. In modern societies, parties both organize representation and express conflict. The judiciary, by contrast, is usually a nonparty institution, as is the professionalized civil service in administrative agencies. The chief executive and cabinet are highly partisan, but usually include only one party (or one coalition).

Visibility

Legislatures as whole bodies are highly visible to the general public, although most individual members are unknown. By contrast, the president or prime minister is the single best recognized person in government, though the larger executive branch itself is unknown to the general public. To the public, the individual members of Congress are lost in the institution, while the institution of the Executive Office of the President is submerged in the personalization of the office.

Legislatures can appear as rowdy meetings in ornate buildings. Because they express conflict, and because their meetings are open to the public, legislatures appear messy, contentious, and argumentative to the public. They can also seem to be overly formalized, ritualized, and time-consuming (Box 1.2).

The other entities of government, instead, hide their internal disagreements. They, too, can be full of conflict. The heated and important battles within the executive branch—for example, over the annual budget—may be the subject of innumerable leaks to the press, but the public never sees the officials engage in actual conflict. Furthermore, there is no public record of who said what to whom, and with what result. There is, likewise, no public record of the confer-

---

Box 1.2

Order in the House

"The House of Commons was never intended to be run like a military establishment. It is a place where emotions sometimes run high, where anger is frequently and legitimately expressed, where Members are entitled to give vent to strong feelings. The Speaker must judge the mood of the House and decide when greater than normal latitude and tolerance are called for. Speaker King expressed the view that . . . the House could never return to the days of an overly authoritarian Speakership."

Laundy 1979, 198

---

ences, much less private discussions, through which judges arrive at their decisions.

By contrast, the legislature is open to public view. Its floor meetings and perhaps committee hearings are televised. All may be publicly available in printed text.

The paradoxical result for legislatures is that the more active they are in expressing societal conflict over public policy questions, the lower their esteem sinks in public opinion. No less a cynic than Bismarck is reputed to have commented that the making of neither laws nor sausage should be seen in public. He had a point. Legislatures in one-party or autocratic countries are reviled for their servility. But in competitive democracies, legislatures are likely to be condemned for the active display of social conflict. In most democracies, legislatures are not highly regarded by the publics who elect them, and whom they represent (Loewenberg and Patterson 1979, 283–88; Norton 1990, 83).

Legislatures are not the only governmental entity that possess any one of these attributes. These characteristics are shared in democracies with other elements of the government. But legislatures are the only institution possessing all attributes together, and they are the one institution that primarily possesses these attributes.

Legislatures and Policy Decisions

To citizens and students who grow up in established democracies, the existence and activity of legislatures are taken for granted. They may be the object of scorn and ridicule, but they are an accepted part of our political structure. In new democracies, however, legislatures are the object of both admiration and wonderment.

Legislatures are especially the object of admiration during periods of dictatorship, military government, or one-party rule. In Central Europe, revitalized parliaments and newly competitive elections to those parliaments were at the top of the reform agenda. Even within the first year of post-communism, however, disenchantment began. While the problems facing these countries were more difficult than anticipated, the difficulties of organizing a newly active legislature proved much more elusive than imagined.

Most countries have some kind of body called "parliament," just as many countries have some kind of popular exercise called "elections." Neither one-party elections of dictatorships nor an inert collection of passive persons called legislatures have much in common with these vital ingredients of democratic self-governance. The German parliament that elected Adolf Hitler, the Russian parliament that got shot at by Boris Yeltsin, and the parliament of Haiti that could not meet because of military suppression all carry the names "parliament" or "legislature" or "national assembly."

The subject of this book—how the world's relatively few democratic legislatures typically are organized and how they function in practice—has become a topic of vital current importance in the new democracies. Both citizens and political elites of the new democracies ask how established democracies get things done.

Only about twenty countries can be considered democratic for most of the period since the end of World War II. They are concentrated in Western Europe and North America, and elsewhere are members of the British Commonwealth. This book necessarily concentrates on that small number of countries, although at the end of the 1980s, waves of democratic transitions occurred first in Latin America and the Mediterranean countries, and then in Eastern Europe.

The place and functioning of legislatures are by no means settled in established democracies, much less in the newer ones. Parliaments at times have been marginalized in the policy-making function to mainly a symbolic role. At times, parliaments have not been sufficiently well organized, nor have their procedures been sufficiently established, to make a larger place for themselves in their political systems.

The major topic to be explored here concerns the factors by which

Table 1.1

Models of Democratic Legislatures

Topics	United States	France	Sweden	Germany	United Kingdom
Chief executive	President	President and premier	Prime minister	Chancellor	Prime minister
Party system	Two-party	Two-coalition	Multiparty	2+ party	Two-party
Legislation	Many bills	Government bills	Government bills	Government bills	Government bills
Committees	Permanent	Few	Permanent	Permanent	Ad hoc bill
	Parallel administrative structure	General	Parallel administrative structure	Parallel administrative structure	Permanent investigation
Floor stage	Independent member votes	Party negotiations	Party negotiations	Party negotiations	Led by minister
Bicameralism	Conference committees	Assembly prevails	Unicameral	Mediation committee	Commons prevails
Veto	Yes	None	None	None	None

parliamentary policy activity is increased. In practical terms, the question becomes: What makes the legislature independent of the executive? What factors help the legislature become autonomous from the chief executive so that it can both defeat proposals from the executive and formulate its own views of proper public policy? Each chapter examines one set of such factors.

The parliaments of democracies appear in three broad groupings (Table 1.1, see page 11). One set consists of the Westminster model, those based upon the British Parliament. The opposite model is mainly confined to one example—the U.S. Congress. They are distinguished initially by their very different relationship to their chief executive, but from that one characteristic, many other differences follow. There is a third set, the parliaments of continental Europe, which occupy a midpoint between the British and U.S. models. We will make frequent reference throughout this book to those three patterns.

Although this discussion has been largely couched in collective terms of the whole institution, legislatures are organizations of people. Our detailed consideration of legislatures begins with the human beings as members.

2

The Members:
Representatives and Legislators

The human beings who populate the legislative institution are that institution's essential raw materials. Their skills, their expectations, and the hopes and fears they bring with them help shape what they do as members. Further, their prior experiences help shape how they adapt, how they learn, and what they contribute to the legislative institution. (For the astounded reaction of one new member of the British Parliament in 1987 to his new work environment, see Box 2.1.) These observations about the members as human beings apply to the staff as well, although we will concentrate on the members themselves.

The human dimension of legislatures is particularly visible and acute in the newly democratized countries. In Central Europe, the anticommunist reformers found themselves, unexpectedly, in parliament as a result of their own success. Not only were they surprised, they were dismayed both at the work load and at the necessity to spend all their time at their new tasks of legislation. As one reformer said, there was only "us" to serve. The only persons with previous experience had served in the old discarded Communist legislature. They were unsuited to a democratic legislature and were repudiated in the new democratic elections.

We will examine the many activities of the members in the legislature, and then will consider the characteristics of the persons who become members.

The Job: Dimensions of Time

The tasks of membership in legislative institutions at the most elemental level consist of time—in two dimensions. First, how much time in a

---

Box 2.1

What Profession Is This?

"The capacity of [British] MPs to cope with the workload and the hours, and be expected to master the detail, is what no one else in any other profession would seriously be asked to do. I was an executive in industry . . . and I would never be expected to do the sorts of tasks and master them."

Quoted in Jogerst 1993, 118

---

day or year does the job take, and second, for how many years do persons remain members?

The Annual Schedule

Legislatures around the world vary from a few days a year to full time. The ceremonial legislatures in dictatorships typically meet seldom. As one new member of a newly democratized legislature of Central Europe observed, their predecessors were violin players in the Communist orchestra. Previously, that legislature met a few days each year, while the newly democratized legislature met every day throughout the entire year. The sheer demands of time were a surprise, usually not a welcome one, to the new democratic reformers.

One characteristic of an inactive legislature, and certainly of an ineffectual one, is that it does not have much time in which to meet. The early British Parliament, for example, "was an event and not an institution" (Russell 1979, 3). The British Glorious Revolution established that "Parliaments ought to be held frequently" (see Box 1.1). They have been ever since.

Most established democratic parliaments meet throughout the year. They may meet several days in the middle of the week, so that the members may be in their districts over a long weekend; time in the district with voters is as much work as meeting in the nation's capital.

Typically, legislatures will adjourn over national holidays and will also observe their nation's summer vacation schedules. For countries with fixed times for elections (e.g., Germany, France, Sweden, the United States), the legislatures adjourn to allow members to campaign for reelection. For countries where elections can be

---

Box 2.2

Privacy?

*Kim Campbell, whose home constituency is in Vancouver, British
Columbia, a continent away from the capital in Ottawa, after her
nomination by the Progressive Conservative Party to be its leader and
the new prime minister of Canada:* "In the course of my life in Ottawa,
my marriage has ended, and I am very far from home. I find life here
often unspeakably lonely and very difficult."

Quoted in the *Boston Globe*, June 20, 1993, 12

---

held at any time (especially Britain and its former colonies), parliament would adjourn quickly as needed for those elections, but
then meet soon afterward to organize the new government.

An immediate consequence for the individuals who become members is that they must acquire full-time living accommodations at the
nation's capital. In small countries, that need is reduced. Some countries, such as Sweden, supply apartments at the parliament for their
members. In others, such as the United States, members typically rent
or purchase homes in Washington, DC, for their families. To travel
frequently between the capital and the district, and to purchase a second home, is a strain on both the time and the finances of the individual members and their families. Life in the capital can also strain
family life (see Box 2.2). The knowledge of these burdens of time,
finance, and family discourages some potential candidates from ever
seriously pursuing national legislative careers.

The Years and Decades of Membership

The legislative term of office varies from two years (United States) up
to five years (Britain) in the lower house. The U.S. Senate, with individual terms of office of six years, has one of the longest terms in
contemporary elected chambers.

The average member of democratic legislatures tends to serve about
ten years in office. Once elected, members tend to run for reelection,
and, as incumbents, they tend to be reelected (see chapter 6 on elections). Often the leadership of legislatures, in both committees and
parties, comes from members with even longer years of service. The

average committee chairperson in the U.S. Congress, for example, has served about twenty years, while the chairpersons of Swedish commit- tees have also served that long (Olson, Pierre, and Piotrowski 1983).

Different length of experience in parliament is itself a source of differing degrees of power. An inexperienced parliament facing a sea- soned executive and administrative structure would be at a disadvan- tage in either responding to proposed legislation or investigating the executive. Within the legislature, the experienced members are more active and effective than are newer and less experienced members. In parliamentary governments, in which the prime minister and cabinet are themselves members of parliament, an inexperienced set of back- benchers, as in Canada, is at a disadvantage in facing a much more experienced set of cabinet members and party leaders (Atkinson and Docherty 1992). The attention to congressional freshmen by American lobbyists on the budget bill in 1993 (Box 2.3) is another example of the liabilities of inexperience.

Membership turnover rates are an attribute both of individual mem- bers and, collectively, of the whole institution. In the U.S. House of Representatives, about half of the membership was in their first term in the middle of the nineteenth century. The proportion of new members slowly decreased until the middle of the twentieth century to about 15 percent (Polsby 1968). In the House elected in 1992, 110 new mem- bers entered (25 percent) out of a total membership of 435. In Canada, the number of new members (out of a total of 295) ranged from a low of 55 newcomers in 1980 to a high of 144 in 1984 (Atkinson and Docherty 1992, 305). In the 1993 Canadian election, with a dramatic change of party majority from Progressive Conservatives to Liberals, over two thirds of the members were freshmen.

The Job: Activities and Roles

Beyond the amount of time, how do members use their time? In what way are the members representatives? In what way are they legisla- tors? What do they do both as representatives and as legislators in their institution with a broad array of potential functions?

Activities

There is no one single answer to these questions. There are many different ways in which any one member can act as "representative."

THE MEMBERS 17

Box 2.3

Whose Experience?

State Legislators in Washington:

"Those who serve in the state legislature are better prepared, they have better command of issues, they know about things: the debate, the compromise, the policy disputes—they are all dealt with in the statehouse."

Member of Congress
Quoted in Berkman 1993, 77

Lobbyists in Washington:

"The freshmen are important, particularly on big issues like the energy tax proposal," said Jerry Jasinowski, president of the National Association of Manufacturers, the lead organization in the American Energy Alliance, a lobbying coalition of more than 1,000 organizations.

"Jack Bonner, head of the lobbying group Bonner & Associates, was more direct. 'The new members tend to be more responsive to our efforts.' "

Comment from Senator Ben Nighthorse Campbell (D-CO), who had previously served in the U.S. House: " 'I was born at night . . . but it wasn't last night.' "

New York Times, July 23, 1993, A1

The member will probably try simultaneously to serve his or her constituents and to act on questions of public policy.

One set of interviews in the 1980s with British MPs found that over two thirds of the members listed "constituency work" as their major job. Only 21 percent, however, found much satisfaction in that type of activity. By contrast, although only 31 percent said they were active in policy matters, having access to the policy-making process was a source of satisfaction to a full 60 percent of the interviewed members (Jogerst 1993, 122–27).

Legislators do many different things; their typical day is divided into rushed little segments. The average German legislator, for example, spends about eight or nine hours per week in plenary, party, and committee work respectively, but their time is also occupied by another twenty discrete activities, the largest of which is travel time to and from their districts (Dalton 1989, 50–51).

Roles

Individual legislators are different from one another; specific legislatures are different from one another. It is genuinely difficult to develop a categorization of types of members that is relevant to most democratic legislatures. Although they all "legislate," and they all "represent," they do so in different ways.

This section therefore presents categories of member behavior and attitudes found in several different democratic legislatures. The varieties of members found in each will help illustrate the broader point about variations among legislatures as well.

British House of Commons

In the early 1970s, about one third of the "backbenchers" were "policy advocates." They, in turn, subdivided into three types. The least common type of member was the ideologist (5 percent). Ideologists would speak of themselves as part of the right wing, or the left, and describe their chief activity as the development and propagation of political ideas. The most common type of policy advocate among backbenchers was the specialist (60 percent). Specialists concentrate on the development of personal knowledge about one specific topic: "If you're going to influence the Executive, you've somehow got to require the senior advisors [to the ministers] to sit up and take notice—and you won't do it by getting bright ideas in your bath." The third category of policy advocate was the generalist (35 percent). Generalists view themselves as well-informed commentators upon current issues, but are not limited to any one issue and its details.

There is a clear connection between these three types of policy advocates and their other identities. Some have selected the topics of their activity because of relevance to their constituency. Others are active on issues because of their own personal backgrounds: a barrister was interested in legal issues, for example, while a physician concentrated on questions of health (Searing 1987).

U.S. House of Representatives

Congressmen describe their activities as concentrating on constituency service and on legislation. They try to blend the best interests of both their district and the nation in their activities. These generalizations about U.S. congressmen as a whole varied, however, with their seniority and experience. First-termers (usually referred to as "freshmen") emphasize the district in their activity and attention, while those with high seniority (six to twelve terms) emphasize legislation as an activity and tend to pay less attention to the district in their thinking about policy questions. This relative shift from district to nation and from district service to legislation may be, in part, a function of the greater electoral safety of senior members over freshmen (Davidson 1969).

This shift can also be regarded as part of the learning experience. While in office, the member learns his or her district, learns how to work with its active citizens and groups, and also learns how to act in office on legislation in ways that are consistent with the policy views and electoral circumstances of the district.

French Chamber of Deputies

French deputies are different from both the British MPs and the American congressmen. They could be placed in four categories based upon their different purposes in entering politics and in running for the National Assembly. The mission participant, the first category, has an ideological mission. A Communist, for example, may be concerned with a "rotten" society that permits mass unemployment, while a Gaullist is concerned with a philosophy "against Fascism, for a worship of man." The second category, the program participants, are immersed in the solution to specific problems such as social security or water systems. They are pragmatists, and unlike the first category, are unconcerned with their political party. The third set, the obligation participants, became involved in politics from a strong sense of moral duty. They do not like politics, and do not enjoy their membership in the Assembly. The fourth and final category of member is the status participant, seeking career advancement beyond, but not in, the National Assembly. Typically, status participants entered politics as staff members to national officials, and joined parties as a means of advancing their careers (Woshinsky 1973).

Experience and Characteristics of Members

There are at least two questions about the members of a legislature. First, what types of people does a legislature need to function effectively in the governing process? And second, what types of people are available within any given society to become members? Both questions imply difficulties in easily achieving a legislature that is either representative or effective.

The types of human beings who could become members of an elected legislature are defined by the intersection of social structure with the political system. Both the social structure and the political system vary among countries, as well as changing over time within any one country.

Society and Politics

The part-time and occasional legislatures over the past 500 years, in those few countries where they were permitted to exist, attracted only those persons with the leisure, or some reason, to participate. Given the slow evolution of legislatures in kingdoms, the right of participation was necessarily high-status. In the occasional and part-time legislatures of the past, members were necessarily employed in other occupations. In seventeenth-century England, they were employed on royal business, as officials of either royal bodies or of local governments (Russell 1979, 3–4).

Over the span of a century, we can see how a changing social structure is reflected, with a time lag, in the membership of legislatures. In the British House of Commons, for example, two thirds of the members came from the landed aristocracy in the 1860s; by 1900, that proportion had declined to 10 percent. In France, the nobility and upper middle class constituted 70 percent of the National Assembly membership in the 1870s; they comprised 20 percent by 1945. Their places were taken mainly by the new urban middle class—lawyers, professionals, and businessmen (Loewenberg and Patterson 1979, 72–73). Simultaneously, the traditional restrictions on the right to vote, on grounds of wealth, race, religion, and gender, have fallen as political systems have democratized (Bailey 1971, 51–55).

The recent experience of the postcommunist countries illustrates the combined impact of social structure with political system. In the absence of private business, of independent labor unions, and of freely organized professions, who in the new democracies was available for political leadership? Writers, dramatists, and artists were, under communist rule, the only occupational groups with the ability to express their own political ideas. Everyone else was employed by the state. Thus, they were the only persons available within their societies to become the new members of revitalized legislatures. The selection of the playwright Vaclav Havel as president of the Czech Republic is an example, as was the emergence of the unemployed electrician Lech Walesa as leader of Solidarity in Poland (Rona-Tas 1991).

Occupation and Education

Comparative legislative research on the members and representation mainly concentrates on the occupational, educational, and social profile of the members. Social structure differs, however, among countries, and in particular the significance of specific occupations varies. Lawyers, physicians, and high school teachers, for example, are very different occupations, with different definitions of status and pay from one country to another. Thus, comparative studies tend to measure generalized categories of high-status, middle-class, and working-class occupational categories.

Today's legislators in democratic political systems tend to be in professional, business, and managerial occupations (Table 2.1). They also come from the major ethnic and religious groups of the society, and are predominately male.

In the United States, we find a large proportion of lawyers and other professional occupations in Congress, persons in "brokerage" occupations. In some other democracies, the proportion of lawyers is much lower in their parliaments simply because the occupation of attorney is different in Europe than it is in the United States.

Members also tend to have university educations. In Germany, for example, about 65 percent of the members of the Bundestag have university educations, and in Britain, 70 percent of the MPs are university-educated (Burch and Moran 1985; Dalton 1989, 186).

With the development of complex societies and complex governments to serve them, we see the growth of a new type of occupation—the professional career in politics. Persons who are employed by

Table 2.1

Occupations of Legislators

	Occupations (%)				
Country Parliament	Professional	Business	Farmer	Manual Worker	Other
U.S. House of Representatives	74	22	3	2	0
U.K. House of Commons	59	29	4	4	4
Swedish Riksdag	56	22	0	7	13
German Bundestag	82	9	6	0	2
Italian Chamber of Deputies	84	4	2	4	7
Japanese House of Representatives	73	14	3	0	11

Source: Loewenberg and Patterson 1979, 70.
Note: Applies mainly to the 1970s.

political parties, interest groups, public relations firms, and legislatures can build a career moving from one employer to another, depending upon their respective political fortunes. This type of person may very well initially seek lower elective office, then work for an interest group or for a legislator, and then run for election to the legislature. In the U.S. House, for example, only 14 percent of representatives were in this category in 1977–78, but that proportion has risen to 20 percent in the House elected in 1992 (*Congressional Quarterly Weekly Report* [hereinafter CQWR] November 7, 1992, 9).

Occupation and education imply not only specific job skills, but also social status, family wealth, and political biases. All during the twentieth century, it has been alleged that the professional and business occupations of legislatures has given those bodies a distinctly conservative bias. Even left-wing parties, however, need competent leadership, and thus their parliamentary membership, too, has become well educated and professional in occupation. Thus, they pride themselves on their working-class family origins. In Germany, for example, almost 30 percent of the Bundestag members had working-class fathers, even though, as we noted above, almost 65 percent had university educations (Dalton 1989, 186).

Religion, Ethnicity, and Gender

Religion can be closely associated with social status, occupations, and political views in any given society. It is ironic that Britain's first (and so far, only) Jew to serve as prime minister was a member of the Church of England. In Western Europe, questions of religious exclusion, a remnant of the wars associated with Protestantism and the Counter-Reformation, are no longer issues in politics. It is in religious affiliation that legislatures are perhaps closest to the profile of the country's population. In Germany prior to unification, for example, about 40 percent of the population was Catholic, while about one-third of the Bundestag members were (Dalton 1989).

Ethnicity, too, is a factor in legislative membership. Ethnic groups that are either low status or few in number tend not to be included in legislatures. Depending on a variety of circumstances, including their geographic concentration, they may slowly become active in local politics and thus also begin to rise in national office. The first immigrant to be elected to Western European parliaments, or to the U.S. Congress, is an event for celebration among the concerned ethnic group. In the U.S. House of Representatives, African Americans gained 9 percent of the seats in 1992, while comprising about 13 percent of the whole population. Hispanics, by contrast, are almost as large a proportion of the population as African Americans, but hold only 4 percent of the House seats (CQWR November 7, 1992, 8). Among a set of six countries, ethnic minorities, however, were overrepresented in four through specific provisions for their inclusion (Lijphart 1986).

Gender has become a visible issue in political participation in democratic societies. The Scandinavian countries have, over the past several decades, had the highest proportion of female parliamentary members —about one-third—while Britain and its former colonies, including the United States, have the fewest (*Economist* February 28, 1987, 47–48; Norris 1987, 114–16).

Political Experience

A different dimension on which to consider legislative members is specifically governmental and political experience. Quite apart from the recent emergence, noted above, of occupational careers in politics, some members bring with them experience in other, and usually "lower," public office. In federations, that relevant experience could be in state legislatures. In the U.S. House of Representatives, for example, 72 percent of the members newly elected in 1992 had served in previous elective office. Likewise, senators frequently have served in statewide elective office, including governor and attorney general. Not all federations are alike, however: MPs in Canada tend not to have previously served in their provincial legislative assemblies (Stewart 1993). That difference in office progression between the two North American federations is a signal of the very ways in which the two federal systems work in practice (Franks and Olson 1993, 24).

All countries, however, have local government. In Britain, the proportion of MPs with local government experience has been increasing from a low of 14 percent in 1945 to a high of 38 percent in 1983 among Conservatives, while about 40 percent and more of Labour MPs during the post–World War II period have local government elective office experience (Burch and Moran 1985).

Some countries permit their MPs to hold two elected offices simultaneously, at different levels of government. Until the 1960s, for example, Sweden permitted its parliamentary members also to serve as local elected public officials (Hancock 1972, 94–95). That dual local-national practice is, if anything, growing in France, so that virtually all members of the parliament simultaneously hold elective local or regional office (Frears 1990, 44–45).

Prior political experience, especially in elective office, does make a difference in how the members of national legislatures, especially newly elected ones, conduct themselves as national representatives and legislators. That interest groups in Washington now target the newly elected freshman members is an indicator that experience literally "counts." That a large proportion of the newly elected freshmen in 1992 had previously held elective office, however, is an indication that they have already experienced lobbyists and their tactics. For views on both the relevant experience of state legislators in Congress and on lobbying of freshmen, see Box 2.3, page 16.

Interest Groups

Some members also have clear affiliations with organized interest groups. This practice is much more common and acknowledged in Europe than in the United States. In Britain, some Labour Party members are "sponsored" by labor unions. They are supported by a labor union for the Labour Party nomination, and they then receive regular salary payments from the sponsoring union while they are in Parliament. This practice began about the turn of the twentieth century, as a means for the labor movement to place working-class members in Parliament. Most Conservative members of Parliament had full-time occupations, and served in Parliament on a part-time and uncompensated basis. In industrial societies generally, it is much easier for a lawyer or physician or businessman to serve part-time in a legislature than it is for a factory worker on an eight-hour-day shift five days a week (and at the turn of the century, it was ten to twelve hours, six days per week; Butler and Kavanagh 1975, 217).

In Germany, almost 60 percent of the Bundestag members had formal links to interest groups. About 12 percent had ties to labor unions, of whom most were members of the Social Democratic Party (SPD). About 14 percent had ties to industry and middle-class organizations, of whom the bulk were members of the Christian Democratic Union (CDU). The largest category of interest groups was the "culture, research, and religious groups," of whom 60 percent were CDU/CSU (Christian Social Union) members, although 26 percent were SPD members (Dalton 1989, 236; Mueller-Rommel 1990, 318–19).

The Upper Chambers

So far, we have discussed mainly the elected members of legislatures. In bicameral systems, this discussion has concentrated on the lower and more powerful elected chamber. United States senators are unusual, for they are directly elected through political parties, and serve in an active and powerful chamber.

The members of upper houses are selected in a wide variety of ways and are correspondingly diverse in their social and even political characteristics. Of twenty-two long-term democratic countries, fourteen were bicameral; the difference was almost entirely a matter of size of population: countries under 10 million tended to be unicameral, while all stable democracies with over 10 million in population had bicameral legislatures. One reason for bicameralism is specifically to represent minorities within the country (Lijphart 1984, 94–98).

While the British House of Lords can be an active chamber on most legislation, it typically is subordinate to the House of Commons, consistent with its nonelective character (Norton 1991, 311–19). Most of

Box 2.4

The House of Lords

David Lloyd George:

"Ordinary men, chosen accidentally from among the unemployed."

The Economist, Nov. 17, 1990, 115.

its members are hereditary aristocracy. A few are "life peers," appointed to the Lords for their lifetime, but their descendants do not inherit the title. Life peers tend to have been active politicians, and have become among the more active of the Lords' members on legislation. As the quote in Box 2.4 indicates, the nonelective character of Lords undermined its ability to be a powerful chamber in a democratic political system.

The Canadian Senate has something of the same irrelevant character because its members are not elected. Although now the object of proposed reforms (Franks 1987), its members have been appointed by the prime minister as a reward for past political service. The patronage and honorific character of the selection has deprived the Canadian Senate of its original intended function of representation of the provinces and regions in Canadian federal government (Watts 1993).

The German Bundesrat, an invention of the post–World War II period, is so far a unique body. It consists of representatives of the provincial governments *(Laender),* with jurisdiction limited to federal questions that involve the provinces. Since the provincial governments are themselves directly elected in provincial elections, their Bundestag delegates have a firm basis in a democratic selection process. Further, since the scope of legislation that affects the provinces is wide, the members of this upper chamber are often involved as active and powerful participants in the development of federal policy (Dalton 1989, 311–12; Loewenberg 1967, 298–305).

The Societal Mirror

It is often claimed, as a criticism, that a legislature is not "representative" because its demographic composition does not closely match the social profile of the population. By that criterion, African Americans and women are underrepresented in the United States Congress, as are also Muslims and the physically challenged. Military veterans and Congregationalists might, by the same criterion, be "overrepresented." This criterion is the "mirror" theory, in which a representative body should reflect the social identities of the society.

Given the geographic division of a country into districts for the election of representatives (with the exception of Israel and the Netherlands), geography is the only attribute of a society that has automatic mirror representation in the legislature. All other characteristics of a society will vary in the extent to which they are reflected in the legislature's composition. In democracies, legislators as well as other political elites come from relatively advantaged, but not the most elite, sectors of society (Aberbach et al. 1981, 47).

The connection between demography and politics, however, is unclear. The politically relevant traits of a population have varied through time and with issues. We have ample examples of how shifting issues change our definitions of who and what should be represented. A century-long agitation for the inclusion of all adult males, irrespective of wealth, is an example, as was the growth of the women's suffrage movement. As life-style issues grow in importance, illustrated currently by abortion-related questions, the personal views and religious outlook of individual legislators can become relevant to how they act and vote on public policy questions (Chressanthis et al. 1991).

Yet, there is always the opposite tendency, that legislators develop a common view as a function of their location in the institutional structure of their political system (see Box 2.5). As a newly elected Canadian MP stated, as Whip of the separatist Bloc Quebecois, "we do not want to make a circus" (*New York Times*, October 31, 1993, A15).

The Members and the Institution

In the long run, there is a "fit" between institution and individual. The legislature and the members adapt to, and reflect, each other. The test of this generalization occurs when a legislature receives an unusually large group of new members, who do not know the institution from the inside, and frequently have criticized it from the outside.

In the U.S. Congress, for example, the large new freshman "classes" of 1964 (LBJ landslide), 1974 (Watergate), and 1992 (Clinton) organ-

Box 2.5

Who Is a Revolutionary?

"Two revolutionaries, only one of whom is a member of parliament, have less in common than two members of parliament, only one of whom is a revolutionary."

Bertrand De Jouvenel
(Quoted in Loewenberg and Patterson 1979, 21)

ized themselves to bring "reform" to the House. Their discontent helped increase the number and power of subcommittees, while reducing the importance of seniority (Davidson and Oleszek 1990, 197–98). In Britain, the new members of the 1960s supplied the discontent that led to the reform of the new committee system in the 1970s (Jogerst 1993, 119).

New members are not only unfamiliar with the routines of an existing institution, they may also bring with them different sets of background experiences. In the British case, the new members beginning in the 1960s were university-educated in white-collar and professional occupations. They were appalled by the working conditions at Parliament, and were frustrated by their lack of both information about and power in government. The MP quoted at the opening of this chapter was one such member. One observer noted in the 1970s, the "mounting frustration among MPs" and that "the younger ones . . . are . . . the most ardent supporters of parliamentary reform" (Ornstein 1981, 38–39; Jogerst 1993, 119).

If experience is a source of expertise and power in a legislature, then a question for the legislature is, how can it attract, and keep, capable members? The recent changes in the British system of departmentally related committees, noted earlier, is an attempt to answer that question. To serve as an ordinary member is, for many active persons, not very attractive over a long period of time. Within parliamentary governments, the avenue of advancement is into the Cabinet, which means rising through the party leadership. As a result, the members are inclined to follow their party leaders, and, assuming the governing party has a majority, parliament acquiesces to the government. Members who do not gain party favor soon leave Parliament.

Box 2.6

The Virtuous Spiral

"New types of Member, trained in the use of words and figures . . . are more likely to be active . . . than were the country gentlemen and retired army officers, on one side [Conservatives—ed.], and the former manual workers and trade-union officials on the other [Labour—ed.] who were the main occupants of their respective backbenches some thirty years ago. Because they are more active . . . more similarly experienced, interested, and active people are attracted to a parliamentary career. It is a virtuous spiral."

Ryle 1988, 229–30

The committee system of the U.S. Congress is a source of satisfaction and career advancement for the members, independent completely from the preferences of the president, and largely independent from the preferences of congressional party leaders. The British system of permanent committees to parallel the structure of the administrative departments now provides for their "backbenchers" an alternative career path to the party and the government. While at least some committee members and chairpersons do later become ministers and party leaders, others find the committees to be a satisfactory means for them to be informed and to be active in the affairs of their government (Jogerst 1993). A close observer of the British MPs noted the "virtuous spiral" between the increase in useful parliamentary activity and the increase in the educational and professional qualification of the members (Box 2.6).

In sum, legislators as individuals and legislatures as whole institutions have many different ways in which they can function as "representatives." The traits of a society that become politically relevant vary through time and among countries. The geographically based districting systems are, so far, the major means discovered by democracies to ensure that, over the long run, society is reflected in parliament. Once elected, the members can think and act in many different ways, illustrated by the British, French, and American ways legislators think of themselves as representatives and legislators.

One of the most important attributes, however, of legislatures is their cumulative experience in the membership. A parliament of too many inexperienced newcomers is likely to be a parliament of dunces; a parliament with not enough newcomers is likely to be a parliament of political fossils. No one knows the proper mix in membership experience to produce a workable balance between political reform and institutional continuity (Atkinson and Docherty 1992, 302). It was a combination in the British Parliament of cumulative membership change and institutional adaptation that produced the "virtuous spiral" of competent members and an active parliament attracted to each other.

3

Political Parties: The Internal Organization of Parliament, I

A legislative assembly is a complicated organization. It usually consists of several hundred members, whose time and work require careful coordination if the legislature is actively to represent its society and to participate in the development of public policy. The two main means by which legislatures organize themselves are through political parties and through committees.

We examine political parties in this chapter, and committees in the following chapter, looking at both as the chief instrumentalities through which both the members and the work of legislatures are organized. We begin with a comparison of parties and committees as different, alternative, and both rival and complimentary means by which the members and work of a legislature are structured.

Parties and Committees Compared

A legislature with many members and a complicated work schedule creates difficult problems of internal organization and leadership. Any king or dictator, or inspired ideological party, will attempt to lead the legislature to do what that external leader wants. If a legislature is to exercise independent judgment on public matters, it requires its own internal leadership structures.

Parties and committees are the two major but different means invented to this point to organize a legislature. Members belong to both types of structures simultaneously, and the interplay between party and committee is an essential feature of each legislature.

In addition to simultaneous membership, there are three specific points at which party and committee intersect in their actions: first, members are placed on committees by their parties; second, committees can be the locale in which parties negotiate their different policy positions with each other as well as with the executive; and third, committees and parties share leadership in floor debate. We will refer to these themes in our discussion here and in chapter 4.

Ordinarily, a legislature will contain only a few political parties, but many committees. The parties tend to be larger, while the committees are smaller. The parties are gatherings of members who, though they usually share a generalized approach to government, differ in their specific subject matter specializations and policy concerns. The committees can be organized by the more specific policy topics of a society, while parties are both more diverse and more generalist.

Political parties lead a contradictory existence. On one hand, they actively seek to win elective office, and to achieve that goal they emphasize their own merits in election campaigns while denigrating the other parties and their candidates. On the other hand, however, within the parliament one of their major tasks is to seek and find agreements with one another.

For the parliament to function, the parliamentary parties must agree on organizational and procedural matters. Often, they must also ultimately agree on policy questions to produce a decision by parliament. In the public arena, and especially at election time, we see the political parties as hostile antagonists, but in parliament, they are frequently cooperative antagonists.

We will examine several aspects of legislative political parties: (1) the party system, (2) the ideological spectrum of parties, (3) party functions in managing and organizing legislatures, (4) the internal organization of the parliamentary parties, and (5) the party relationship with its external units and with the chief executive.

Party Systems

The number and relative sizes of the political parties in parliament are indicated by the term "party system." The conventional categories are indicated simply by numbers: A one-party system is usually found in dictatorships or Third World countries. Democratic systems, with competitive elections, produce at least two parties (two-party system) or many parties (multiparty system). Examples of two-party and multi-party systems are shown in Tables 3.1 and 3.2.

Within democratic legislatures, if one party has a majority of seats, it can often unilaterally make decisions on public policy. In parliamentary systems, as opposed to a dual branch system, the majority party selects the prime minister and holds most if not all seats in the cabinet. In parliamentary systems, power is usually transferred to the Government of the Day from the parliament. Leadership of the majority party is also transferred from the party itself to the cabinet. The main task of the majority party is to defend the cabinet and its policies, while the main task of the minority is to decide if, when, and how to attack.

A single majority party is much easier to form in a two-party system than in a multiparty system. In the latter, the many parties divide the electorate into small units, none of which is likely to obtain a majority (see Table 3.2). In the extreme case—illustrated by Belgium, the Netherlands, Italy, and at one time, France and Sweden—government instability was a constant fact of life. Because there was no continuing government to control parliament, no one party or combination of parties could control parliament either. The result was not parliamentary power, but parliamentary immobilism and indecision. The specter of growing fragmentation of parties during the Weimar Republic resulting in the Hitler regime, and the prospect of constant instability in France after World War II, led both countries to adopt constitutional provisions that limit both the number and the power of parliamentary parties. The examples of both countries have had a powerful effect on the thinking of subsequent democratic constitution writers: their goal has been to avoid party fragmentation (Ehrmann and Schain 1992; Neumann 1956).

Numerous legal restrictions have been invented to limit the number and fragmentation of parties. The most common is the vote "threshold," specifying that parties must obtain 3 to 5 percent of the vote to qualify to win seats in parliament. This and other electoral law provisions are discussed in chapter 6. The most draconian constitutional provision yet invented to curb party fragmentation is the requirement in the 1989 Nigerian constitution that "There shall be only 2 political parties" (Sec. 220.1), now named the Social Democratic Party and the National Republican Convention, one "a little" to the left, the other equally but no more to the right (Ademolekan 1991).

As contemporary Germany and France illustrate, there are many

Table 3.1

Two-Party Systems in Britain, the United States, and Canada: Seats in the Legislature

Party	British House of Commons (1992) N	%	Party	U.S. House of Representatives (1992) N	%	Party	Canadian House of Commons (1988) N	%
Conservative	336	51.61	Democratic	258	59.31	Progressive Conservative	170	57.63
Labour	271	41.63	Republican	176	40.46	Liberal	82	27.80
Liberal Democrats	20	3.07	Other	1	.23	New Democrats	43	14.58
Scottish National	3	.46						
Welsh Nationalist	4	.61						
Ulster Unionist	9	1.38						
Democratic Unionist	3	.46						
Ulster Popular Union	1	.15						
Social Democratic, Labor	4	.61						
Total	651	100.00		435	100.00		295	100.00

Table 3.2

Multiparty Systems: Seats in Parliament

German Bundestag (1987)[a]			Swedish Riksdag (1988)[b]			Italian Chamber of Deputies (1983)[c]		
Party	N	%	Bloc and Party	N	%	Party	N	%
			Nonsocialist					
Christian Democrats*	223	44.87	Moderate	66	18.91	Chistian Democrats*	225	36.00
						Republican*	29	4.64
Free Democrats*	46	9.26	Liberal	44	12.61	Liberal*	16	2.56
			Center	42	12.03			
			Socialist					
Social Democrats	186	37.42	Socialist*	156	44.70	Social Democrats	23	3.68
						Socialist*	73	11.68
			Communist	21	6.02	Communist	198	31.68
			Other					
Greens	42	8.45	Greens	20	5.73	Fascist	43	6.88
						Radical	11	1.76
						Left	7	1.12
Total	487	100.0	Total	349	100.0	Total	625	100.0

Sources: [a] Dalton (1989, 283); [b] *Current Sweden*, no. 385 (October 1991); [c] Sassoon (1986, 167).

Notes: Parties listed in parallel with Swedish bloc formation.

* Parties that formed the government after election.

variations in the number and size of parties within the very broad "multiparty" designation. Germany has been called a "2 and 1/2" party system, for the number of parties and their relative sizes have stabilized at two large ones (about 35 percent to 45 percent of the vote each) and one small one (about 10 percent). The many French parties have consolidated to four large ones, which in turn tend to form two stable coalitions (Wilson 1989). Perhaps we should term contemporary Germany and France as "several-party" systems.

Germany and France have seen in the post–World War II era a gradual consolidation of parties, while Scandinavia in the 1980s has experienced increasing fragmentation. For decades, Scandinavian countries have been examples of stable government in a multiparty system. The dominance of the Social Democrats, from the depression era of the 1930s into the 1960s, provided stable government. Although the Social Democratic parties usually lacked a clear majority, each was much larger than any of its competitors, so that support from one or two smaller parties was sufficient to form and support a cabinet. The number of parties in parliament has increased in the 1980s, and the difficulties in forming a stable majority government have correspondingly increased (Damgaard 1992, 194–95; Elder et al. 1982, 85–99; Hancock 1993).

In dual-branch systems, however, the number of parties and their relative size within the legislature are ordinarily irrelevant to the selection of the president. The internal party system can affect how the legislature reacts to presidential proposals, but neither the selection nor the tenure in office of the president is affected by the party system within Congress. In the United States, Republican presidents since the end of World War II have faced Democratic Congresses, while in France, a Socialist president has experienced conservative majorities in the National Assembly. In both French instances, the Socialist president has appointed, in keeping with the legislative majority, a conservative premier (Ehrmann and Schain 1992, 322–24).

Party systems have a major impact on the relationship between the cabinet and the parliament. In parliamentary systems, the "several-party" systems increase the autonomy of parliament from the executive. In dual-branch systems, the constitutional structure protects legislative parties from executive dominance, but it does not guarantee such independence.

The Ideological Spectrum

In industrial democracies, political parties are usually arrayed along a left–right continuum, based upon economic policy differences. The main political parties of democratic Western Europe may be grouped into five broad categories as conservative, liberal, center, socialist, and communist (Peters 1991, 145–53; *Economist* November 23, 1991, 59–60). They are discussed below on a right-to-left socioeconomics issues continuum.

The conservative parties of Western Europe have a variety of names (Moderate Unity in Sweden, Peoples Party in Austria), though many on the continent employ the name "Christian," as for example, the Christian Democrats in Germany and in Italy. By and large, they have supported the European tendency toward a mixed or social-market economy, but have also attempted to limit wage increases, and have had the support of the business communities of their countries. In the 1980s, under the combined influences of Thatcher and Reagan, conservative parties have adopted the rhetoric of the small state and of market forces.

Liberal parties in Europe, unlike the term in the United States, refer to economically conservative parties which, in addition, have a strong commitment to civil liberties and to anti-clericalism in state–church relations. The description "liberal" refers to their nineteenth-century origins against the rural aristocracy and established state churches. Their current names include People's Party (Sweden) and Free Democrats (Germany).

In this description of ideological tendencies, we have begun with parties on the "right." Others define themselves as "center" parties. They are heterogeneous in their different national origins, having a rural and Protestant nonconformist base in Scandinavia, for example. Currently, they try to find common ground between left and right parties, and consequently, often serve in coalition governments.

Socialist parties most commonly are called social democratic. They early adopted the term "democratic" to sharply distinguish themselves from communists. Just as conservative parties tend to have business support, socialist parties have worker support, especially that of organized labor. In Britain, the socialist party is called the "Labour Party."

Communist parties have usually been excluded from Western European cabinets on the grounds that they were "antisystem" parties. They have tended to be small (Italy is the major exception; see Table 3.2, page 35), and to become increasingly diverse with the approach of the end of the Cold War. Beginning in the 1970s, several explicitly adopted a "Euro-communism" stance, in which they separated themselves from the Soviet Union and discarded the Leninist ideological basis of their party. The Italian Communist Party was the most reformist, while the French was the least.

Socialists and conservatives have tended to be the largest parties of their countries, with each set having formed their governments during most of the post–World War II period.

This simplified set of five party groups has always been threatened by other parties, and by the growth in the 1980s of parties concerned with other types of issues. Economic policy is not the only source of differences among parties, either now or in the past, nor do people vote only on economic criteria (Lewis-Beck 1988, 83–85). Until democracy was firmly established in most European countries—that is, until the end of World War I—democracy itself was one of the main sources of disagreement among parties. As part of that set of issues, the parties differed in their concern for civil liberties, religious toleration, and the right to vote (LaPalombara and Weiner 1966).

New parties form continually, and some of them place members in parliament. In particular, the "postindustrial" issue parties are a new party formation, best illustrated by the "Greens," the environmental protection parties in Germany and Sweden that arose in the 1970s. In the new postcommunist era of Central Europe in the 1990s, the many ethnic groups contained within single countries sometimes form their own political parties, raising questions both of equal treatment and even of the creation of new states. In addition, the growth of the European Common Market has introduced severe disagreements within existing parties.

A common view of political parties is that they have a specific source of support within the social and economic structure of society, and that they have clear statements of policies, perhaps based upon or justified by an ideology.

There is, however, a very different concept of party: the broad, diffuse, vote-attracting party (Kirchheimer 1966). In Europe, perhaps the Christian Democratic Union/Social Christian Union of Germany is the best example, while the American parties are also illustrations of the "catch-all party," or "Volkspartei." The Austrian parties are also examples (Mueller 1992). One difficulty facing the British Labour Party is that its relatively clearly focused program repelled, rather than attracted, its potential voters in the 1980s (*New York Times* January 23, 1993). To appeal to a large number of voters approaching a majority in the modern complex and diverse state perhaps requires a diverse party in its internal composition, and a vague and broad statement of policy objectives in its electoral campaign.

We now turn to the tasks of parliamentary parties and to their internal organization. We will also review the extent and variations in party voting and discipline.

Organization of the Chamber

Parties are responsible for the organization of the members and of the whole chamber. Members usually sit in the chamber by party, chamber officers and committees are selected by parties, and parties raise and resolve organizational and procedural issues.

Seating on the Floor

The seating arrangement in legislatures is the origin of the terms *left* and *right* to designate political tendencies. In the assemblies of the French Revolution, the most radical members sat to the presiding officer's left; those most opposed to them sat, in the semicircular chamber, as far away as they could get, to the right (Harrison and Sullivan 1980, 484). Continental parliaments still tend to retain this left–right gradation in seating arrangements on the floor, the physical geography of which is well suited to multiparty systems.

Westminster parliaments retain the distinctive British pattern of two sets of benches that face each other from opposite sides of a long rectangular hall. During debate, when one member refers to another as "the Member opposite," he or she literally is referring to the seating arrangement in the chamber, as well as to their political relationship (Figure 3.1).

The two opposed sets of benches both express, and some would say help shape, the British "two-party" system. British legislative geography also is the origin of the term "crossing the floor" when an MP changes party membership. Winston Churchill became an expert on the British two-party system by crossing the floor not once, but twice, beginning and ending as a Conservative, with an interlude on the Liberal Party benches (Box 3.1).

Figure 3.1. **Floor Plan of British House of Commons**

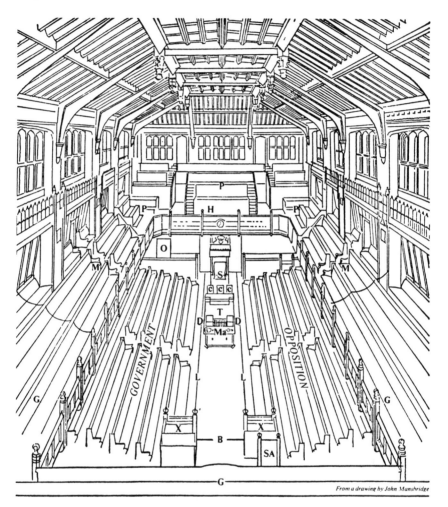

From a drawing by John Munsbridge

S	Mr Speaker	T	Table of the House	SA	Serjeant at Arms
P	Press Galleries	D	Despatch Boxes	M	Members' Galleries
H	*Hansard* Reporters	Ma	Mace†	G	Visitors' Galleries
O	Government Officials' Box	L	Lines‡		
	(advisers to Ministers)	B	Bar of the House		
C	Clerks of the House*	X	Cross Benches		

*When the House goes into Committee, the Speaker leaves the Chair, and the Chairman sits in the chair of the Clerk of the House, which is the one on the left.   †When the House goes into Committee, the Mace is put 'below the Table' on brackets.   ‡Lines over which Members may not step when speaking from the front benches.

Box 3.1

Churchill on the Shape of the Party System

*When debating how the chamber of the House of Commons should be
reconstructed after World War II air raid damage, Winston Churchill,
then war-time prime minister, argued:*

"Its shape should be oblong and not semi-circular. . . . It is easy for an
individual to move through those insensible gradations from Left to Right
[in a semi-circular chamber] but the act of crossing the Floor is one
which requires serious consideration. I am well informed on that matter,
for I have accomplished that difficult process, not only once but twice.
Logic is a poor guide compared with custom."

House of Commons Debates, October 28, 1943
(Quoted in Franks 1987, 144)

Most parliaments specify the legal conditions in their standing orders
for the formation of a legislative party, called "Fraktion" in Germany, and
termed "Klub" in some European countries. The essential criterion is size:
a party group must have a designated minimum number of members to be
recognized as a party club. Such recognition entitles that group of members to participate in the formal organization decisions of the parliament.

Chamber Officers

One essential task of legislative parties is to select the presiding officer of
the chamber. In multiparty parliaments in which the cabinet is formed by
interparty negotiation, the presiding officer ("Speaker" in Britain and the
United States) is one of the offices allocated among the participating
parties. In the U.S. House of Representatives, the Speaker is selected by
the majority party, and is usually the leader of the majority party. In
Britain, Speakers traditionally are nonpartisan in the exercise of their
office, although they, too, are selected by the majority party (Laundy
1979). The Speaker selected by the British House of Commons in 1992,
Betty Boothroyd, is the first woman to occupy that high-status and powerful position. Her selection also marked the first time that a member of
the minority party was selected by the majority party for that office.[1]

---

[1] I am indebted to Michael Ryle for this historical note.

Box 3.2

The Speaker Speaks

Reply of the Speaker when the king and troops invaded a meeting of Parliament in 1640, demanding to know whether several members, whom he was going to arrest, were present:

"May it please your Majesty, I have neither eyes to see nor tongue to speak in this place, but as the House doth direct me, whose servant I am."

Bailey 1971, 62

The very name, "Speaker," illustrates the tortured and long path by which legislatures became independent of kings. The designation of "Speaker" indicated the member of Britain's Parliament appointed by the king to report back to him the activities inside Parliament. Only slowly did Parliament gain control over that office, making it the leading symbol of its independent authority against the king, his wishes, and his armies. The most famous single episode in that long history is shown in Box 3.2.

Schedule and Procedures

Most decisions about the flow of legislation to the floor are made by interparty discussions. In continental multiparty parliaments, the interparty negotiation committee is often termed something like a "Committee of Elders" (Loewenberg 1967, 202–6), while in the simpler two-party system of Britain, the party officers informally confer "behind the chair," that is, off the floor at a convenient location which in fact is behind the Speaker's chair (see Figure 3.1, page 40).

Structure of Chamber Committees

Committee seats are usually distributed in accordance with party size in the chamber. In parliamentary systems, a majority-based government will control a majority of committee seats. But if the government is a minority, that government will face committees largely controlled by opposition parties.

Parties also decide on the allocation of committee chairpersons among the parties. In the United States, the majority party automatically holds all committee and subcommittee chairs. In two-party Britain, some committees are traditionally chaired by members of the opposition party. In multiparty continental parliaments, committee chairs and vice-chairpersons are carefully shared among the several parties proportional to their strength in the chamber. The party leaders negotiate how many and which committee leadership positions will go to each party. It is then up to each party to decide internally who among its members will get those committee positions.

Party Officers

Legislative parties are complicated organizations. They can have several hundred members, which presents major and continuing problems of internal coordination and decision making. If a legislative party is relatively small, however, it pays the penalty of not having enough members to attend to the busy life of the legislature. Each party selects its own leaders and most parties also manage their internal affairs through a set of party committees. The party's capacity to organize and manage its internal affairs is a powerful factor in the development and protection of the parliament's autonomy from the chief executive.

Party Leader

Party leaders are prominent in floor sessions. They often sit in specific locations, and are accorded preferential recognition by the chair. Because of the seating arrangements in Westminster parliaments, party leaders sit in the first row of benches on each side, while the ordinary members sit behind them, leading to the terms "front bench" for party leaders and "back bench" for other members of the party in parliament.

Most parliamentary parties select their leader through an internal election, which can become every bit as complicated as a full election by the electorate (Norton 1979, 49–59). In most parliamentary systems, the party's leader is also that party's nominee for prime minister, and thus the office itself of party leader, and its selection process, are of great importance.

The high-stakes character of party leadership was illustrated in Britain in 1990, when Margaret Thatcher, the prime minister, was removed from that office and replaced by John Major. That change in the office of chief executive did not occur through a vote on the floor by the House of Commons. Rather, she was removed as party leader by a vote of only those MPs who were members of the Conservative Party. It was a party decision, not a House decision (*Financial Times* November 23, 1990). She had, however, become Conservative leader fifteen years earlier by defeating, in an internal party selection, the incumbent in that position. Having become the Conservative leader, Margaret Thatcher had become that party's nominee for prime minister; she then lost the office of prime minister in the same way.

Canada and Germany, however, reverse the process. Their parliamentary party leaders are elected initially in party conventions, similar to U.S. presidential nominating conventions. Once selected outside of Parliament, if those leaders are not already in Parliament, they join Parliament and become their party leaders within Parliament. In the instance of the Canadian selection of Kim Campbell as party leader and thus also as prime minister by the party national convention in 1993, she was already a member of the parliament and cabinet (*Boston Globe* June 20, 1993).

Party leaders tend to be moderates within their own parliamentary party. Margaret Thatcher was a clear exception to this generalization, which perhaps helps explain the circumstances of her removal. Major parties in complex societies tend to be diverse in both composition and policy preferences. An essential task of a "leader" is to find compromises within the party that will win partywide support.

An essential task of party leaders is to negotiate with the other parties and their leaders. There is often, however, disagreement within any one party about how accommodating its leaders should be in their relationships with the other parties and their leaders. In the U.S. House of Representatives, for example, Republican leader Robert Michel was increasingly criticized by a new generation of "Young Turks" within his own party in the 1980s (Box 3.3).

In parliamentary systems, it is common for opposition parties to form a "shadow cabinet," to use a British term. The Labour Party, in opposition for over a decade, has designated each of its leaders to follow the activities of one government minister. When a minister speaks on the floor, the opposition "front bench spokesman" will also speak for his party. When the Conservatives formed the government in 1979, several of the new ministers had most recently been their party's

Box 3.3

Perils of the Minority

Rep. Robert Michel, House Republican leader since 1978, announced he would retire from the House after the 1994 election, clearing the way "for the more combative style personified by Representative Newt Gingrich of Georgia."

Michel said that the House "today lacked 'comaraderie' and complained of House members who indulge in 'trashing the institution.'"

This comment was directed "at new members who won election by attacking Congress. . . . Mr. Gingrich's political action committee, Gopac, trained Republican candidates last year to attack Congress."

Adam Clymer, "Michel, House GOP Leader, to Retire Next Year," *New York Times*, Oct. 5, 1993

"Michel's departure . . . marks the end of an era. Like his predecessors in the minority leadership, Gerald R. Ford of Michigan and John J. Rhodes of Arizona, he is part of the generation of World War II veterans who remade politics in their home towns . . .

"All three were picked for seats on the Appropriations Committee . . . a panel that values hard workers with a willingness to compromise, and abhors publicity-seekers and bomb-throwers . . .

"Michel stayed on, increasingly isolated among House Republicans elected in the 1980's and 1990's, who came with a harder edge to their conservatism and a television-bred liking for tough, partisan one-liners.

"He has lost on countless . . . roll calls since he came to the House at the start of Dwight Eisenhower's second term. . . . He will depart knowing that . . . he has strengthened—and not undermined—the institution in which he has served."

David S. Broder, "Bob Michel and the Virtues of Moderation," *Washington Post*, Oct. 10, 1993

shadow ministers to monitor the Labour ministers then in power, some of whom then became their "shadow ministers."

The relationship between party leaders on the front bench and their backbench followers in a legislature is always sensitive. Thus, each party has a complicated internal organization, including the "whip" and often also a set of internal party committees.

Whip

The formidable name "whip" refers to those party officers who are responsible for two critical tasks: agreement between the parties on a schedule for the chamber, and attendance and voting by the party deputies (Norton 1979).

The schedule of legislative activity—when bills come to the floor and even the timing of a specific floor vote—is often decided by discussions among party leaders. The party whip has special responsibility for scheduling and procedural decisions between the parties. Although the majority party or government coalition has the major responsibility to decide which bills come to the floor, the minority and opposition parties are regularly consulted on the timing of action on government matters. Since the government party would be willing to have its bills accepted without either debate or roll call voting, the initiative rests with the opposition to schedule time for debate and for the time-consuming methods of roll call voting.

The whip also monitors members' attendance and works to ensure that the party members vote in accordance with party policy. In Britain, the "whip notice" lists the schedule of bills on the floor. Each bill can be underlined on the printed notice, indicating the degree of importance of the bill to the party leadership. The highest importance is indicated by three lines under the bill's title on the paper. Members are expected to vote with their party on any "three line whip" as a matter of party discipline.

In large parties, a "chief whip" has a structure of assistant whips, usually apportioned regionally among the party members. The assistant whips have the daily responsibility of talking with party members with the dual assignment to ensure member attendance and votes but also to know member thinking and to communicate those views upward to party leaders and, in the case of parties in the cabinet, to government leaders as well.

Party Committees

Legislative parties vary greatly in the extent and density of their internal structure. The parliamentary parties of Germany and Sweden, for example, have elaborate committee structures to cover all fields of public policy. Party views are developed within their party committees, and then are considered in the full meeting of the party deputies.

For parties in government, the internal legislative party committees are a means of communication with and sometimes protest against the decisions of their own party's government. For the opposition, this structure of committees is a means of developing their own views of public policy against those of the government. In both sets of legislative parties, their internal committee leaders are able to negotiate with each other to explore the possibility of compromise solutions (Isberg 1982; LeLoup and Woolley 1991, 51; Loewenberg 1967, 191–202). The leaders of the party subject matter committees usually hold their party's seats on the parallel chamber committees. Thus, the legislative committee (discussed in chapter 4) often serves as a place where party leaders meet and explore the options of interparty agreement.

The British and American legislative parties are not nearly as strongly organized as in other democracies. In Britain, the party committees are open forums of interested members, but not decision-making groups. Conservative MPs have used internal party committees in an attempt to modify government policy, while in the Labour Party, attendance is very low (Norton 1979, 32–49; Norton 1988, 114–16; Searing 1987, 440).

In the U.S. Congress, both parties sometimes form "task forces" or ad hoc working groups to develop a party view on new important issues. When industrial policy, and then later, issues of international trade became important during the Reagan administration, for example, both congressional parties formed working groups and task forces in efforts to develop a partywide view on a relatively new but controversial issue (Olson et al. 1991). In anticipation of the Clinton administration's health care proposals, House and Senate Republicans formed several informal working groups to monitor the proposal preparation steps within the administration (*Wall Street Journal* May 21, 1993, A12; *New York Times* September 23, 1993, A12; and CQWR September 18, 1993, 2456).

Party Member Meetings

Party members in a legislature may meet as a whole body. The terms used to describe such a partywide meeting vary among countries and

---

Box 3.4

The Rapture of Party

British Prime Minister John Major was dropping in the public opinion polls, his party was badly split over the Common Market, and he had just fired Norman Lamont from the cabinet as chancellor of the Exchequer. Lamont had then delivered a severe attack upon the Prime Minister from his new place on the backbenches.

In response, a "carefully crafted statement . . . by the Executive of the 1992 committee, the senior group of Tory MPs, . . . agreed [to] unanimously, offered the prime minister '100 per cent support.' Speaking after the weekly meeting of Conservative MPs, Sir Marcus Fox, chairman of the committee, said the statement had won a 'rapturous reception' from the 150 or so backbenchers present."

Financial Times, June 11, 1993

---

parties. The Parliamentary Labour Party and the "1922 Committee" are terms used in Britain for Labour and Conservatives, respectively (Norton 1979, 21–31). In the U.S. Congress, the Democrats meet in "caucus," while the Republicans meet in "conference." The Canadian party meetings are also the "caucus."

The frequency and importance of legislative party meetings vary greatly among countries. In most countries, the parties meet at the beginning of a new legislature and at the beginning of a new session for organizational purposes. There is a wide variety of practices for discussions of and decisions about party views on policy questions. In Britain and the United States, the legislative parties meet infrequently, while in Germany and Sweden, they meet on a regular schedule every week. In the U.S. House, however, the caucuses of both parties are becoming more active (Hammond 1991).

Party meetings are the forum in which party leaders are elected. Party meetings are also the proper authority for deciding party views on policy matters, and thus they also decide the issues on which members are expected to vote with the party on the chamber floor. Party meetings can also be cheerleading sections, as illustrated by the British Conservatives' "1922 Committee" when Prime Minister Major got in trouble (Box 3.4).

Most legislative party meetings are held in secret. Neither the public nor the press is admitted, and no official record of proceedings is released. While the official actions of legislatures are conducted in public, as stressed in the opening chapter, the more important internal party decisions are conducted privately. The more important the meetings, the greater the public criticism of the secrecy. The importance of the German "Fraktion" parliamentary party and its secret meetings has led to much more public criticism, for example, than the equally secret but much less important meetings of the U.S. congressional parties.

Party Discipline

The term "party discipline" means that a party's legislators are required to vote with their party on those matters that the party has defined as important to it.

Few policy statements are adopted by the U.S. congressional party meetings. The parties neither pronounce nor enforce party discipline. While members usually do want to vote with their party, they are entirely free to vote differently, and usually show less party cohesion than is found in other democratic legislatures. Compared with other democracies, the U.S. Congress has "party-free" voting.

Party discipline is enforced in Britain through the elaborate whip structure. The party view, however, is much more defined by the party leadership—either the governing cabinet or the opposition's "shadow cabinet"—than by the party membership through an internal structure of decision making and committees.

The continental parliamentary parties are usually strongly led and highly cohesive. Once a party position has been defined through the internal committees and the partywide meeting, members are expected to vote and speak in support of that view. Members willingly join their parties, and do believe in the positive values of development and acting in accordance with partywide views. The exercise of sanctions or punishment against members in democratic legislatures is rarely used, and rarely needed.

When party discipline is exercised by the governing party or party coalition, and that group holds a majority of seats, the position of the government will be supported by the governmental party majority on all floor votes. In Germany, for example, while the number of roll calls has been over one hundred in some sessions, the number of government defeats has never exceeded five per session (Saalfeld 1990, 73–75).

However, when the cabinet is supported by a minority of members of parliament, party discipline can be invoked against the government. Thus, a minority government has every reason to attempt to negotiate a compromise with other parties to form a policy position that a majority will support. Several minority governments in Sweden, for example, had much less legislative success in Riksdagen than had majority governments. The minority governments would adopt compromises with different parties, depending upon the issue (Isberg 1982).

Party Voting

Most votes and decisions in legislatures are noncontroversial. Either the legislature pursues continuing routine matters, or agreements have been negotiated in advance. Only a minority of decisions are brought to a vote, and only a small portion of them are highly controversial and contested.

Any cabinet routinely submits continuation items to the legislature for approval, and once reviewed by internal party groups and chamber committees, these will be routinely cleared on the floor. Approximately 70 percent of all government bills in the British Parliament, for example, are approved without a formal vote (Norton 1988, 101–02). Although some 400 roll call votes are held in each chamber of the U.S. Congress annually, only a dozen or so votes are designated as "key" votes for the year (Seligman 1979).

Party Cohesion, Rebellion, and Loyalty

Most studies of roll call voting in the U.S. Congress examine the extent and correlates of party-loyal voting (Cox and McCubbins 1991). Most studies in Britain, by contrast, examine the extent and correlates of party rebellion. The difference in terminology reflects the underlying different reality of the two democratic legislative systems (Epstein 1967, 318–48).

Most studies of roll call voting in continental European parliaments examine the cleavage structures among political parties. Their unit of analysis is not how individual members vote, for all vote with their party; it is the party, not the individual member, that becomes the action unit in party-loyal multiparty democratic legislatures. In the Norwegian Storting, for example, the several parties vote with and against each other on a left–right continuum of issues; a new set of environmental and life-style issues is, however, slowly becoming important (Shaffer 1991, 59–80). During the 1960s, Swedish parties voted with each other in varying combinations depending upon the issue, reflecting similar party patterns from before World War II (Bjurulf 1972; Stjernquist and Bjurulf 1970).

British thinking about party voting in Parliament has changed considerably in the past two decades, largely because voting practices have changed. Britain had a minority Labour government during much of the 1970s, and also had an increasingly divided Conservative Party in opposition. During that unusual time—unusual at least in this century—members of both parties increasingly voted against their party, and even the government lost votes, especially on amendments. But, as will be discussed in chapter 5, the government did not "fall." One of the main arguments for party loyalty thus did not apply. Nevertheless, British MPs hold a strong sense of loyalty to their party, and almost invariably vote with their party leadership (Mughan 1990; Norton 1988, 112–14).

The Canadian Parliament illustrates the party loyalty extreme of which the Westminster model is capable. Every vote in that parliament is regarded as a "confidence" vote, and thus every MP is required to vote with his party as a "trained seal." There are no deviations. At least some members feel very unhappy at the party restraint under which they work, and proposals have been advanced to help the ordinary member become more active. One of the proposals, not accepted by the leadership of any party, is to relax the definition of a "confidence" vote (Franks 1987, 99–115; Stewart 1991, 53–54).

German legislators also sometimes feel overly constrained by government and party. Over 180 members have actively sought parliamentary reform to increase opportunities both for individual members and for small parties to act (Saalfeld 1990, 75–81). A dramatic example of a "party-free" vote was the decision about relocation of the capital from Bonn to Berlin following reunification of the state (*Frankfurter Allgemeine Zeitung* June 21, 1991).

The extent of party voting in the U.S. Congress is usually measured by the 50 percent rule—those votes on which a majority of each party vote oppositely are defined as "party votes." By that measure, the frequency of party voting has ranged, over the past several decades in the House, from a low of 27 percent during the Nixon administration to a high of 55 percent during the Bush administration. Although party voting has been increasing in the U.S. Congress, no other democratic legislature shows such low levels of party voting. The contrast between "party-free" voting in the United States and "party-loyal" voting in all other democratic parliaments is a real one, but it is not absolute.

Factionalism

Few political parties are completely united in action and fully agreed on policy. As parties successfully appeal for votes in democratic elections, and as they become larger, they also become more heterogeneous in composition and diverse in policy views.

Among social democratic parties in Europe, the most divisive question has often concerned the extent of social services and of nationalization of industry. Among the nonsocialist parties, the most divisive issues have involved the amount and extent of taxation and the extent of social services. As the Common Market has grown and developed in Europe, several parties, especially the two major ones in Britain, have developed severe internal disputes over affiliation with and participation in the Common Market. In chapter 6, we will note the adventures of Prime Minister John Major in facing the "Euro-sceptics" within his own party in mid-1993.

Roll call voting on the floor is a much more visible sign of internal party factionalism in the U.S. Congress than in other democratic parliaments, given the latter's usual emphasis upon party discipline at the floor stage. Their internal party divisions are most visible in the conflicting statements by party leaders and MPs, and in their platform disputes at national party conventions.

In U.S. congressional parties, Southern Democrats have been the single most visible large faction within either party. Developed initially during the New Deal in the late 1930s, this faction's core concern had been the continuance of racial segregation in the southern states. It also developed a strong conservatism on economic issues as well. For three decades following World War II, Southern Democrats voted with Republicans, forming the "Conservative Coalition." It was most active and also successful in floor votes during the Nixon administration, which, as noted above, was also the time of lowest party voting in

Congress. Since then, however, the Republican Party has grown in the South, the South has accepted civil rights changes, and Democrats who run for and are elected to Congress from the South increasingly think and vote like national Democrats. While there are still regional differences among Democrats in Congress, there is now a growing regional difference among national Republicans as well. The House has formed several formal "caucuses," which tend to function as factional groups within parties, of which the Democratic Study Group (DSG) is the most visible; it was created largely to combat Southern Democratic factionalism in the 1960s (Ripley 1983, 254–59).

If differences within a party become intense, one option is for a group to withdraw from the party and form a new one. In the 1980s, for example, several prominent Labour MPs formed their own new party, the Social Democrats, sat together as a party in Parliament, and ran candidates in the next general election. They have since split, and merged with the former Liberal Party to form the new Liberal Democratic Party (Norton 1991, 150–55).

The Liberal Democratic Party in Japan, continuously in government for the past forty years, is structured on a set of factions. One of them, however, voted against its own party's prime minister in a vote of no confidence in 1993. That faction then ran candidates in the next election as its own new party. This episode is discussed in chapter 5.

No democratic legislative party is completely in agreement on all matters. Even if the members largely agree on an existing set of issues, new issues always threaten to erupt, presenting the parties with new challenges to find and keep interparty agreement. In these respects, each legislative party is a mini-legislature, facing the same problems of building agreement and unity out of disagreement and disunity. Within parties, this problem is termed "factionalism"; within legislatures, this problem is termed "partisanship."

External Links

Political parties, unlike chamber committees, are organized both inside the legislature and outside at countrywide and constituency levels. The relationship between the legislative and external units of the same party is another matter on which countries and individual parties vary greatly.

The British Labour Party has recently experienced a twenty-year struggle for control between the external organizations and the parliamentary party. Usually, left-wing parties assert that the members and officers outside the parliament should define what the legislative unit should do, while center and right-wing parties usually do not make that claim (Epstein 1967, 289–314).

The usual pattern, however, is that most party decisions in parliament are made through the legislative party structures and officers discussed above. Furthermore, the legislative party leaders are usually also the leaders of the external party organizations. The practice of external selection of the party's parliamentary leader, also discussed above, is simultaneously a potential means of unifying diverse elements of the party and a potential source of increased conflict between the legislative and external units of the party.

The external party is at least a potential source of constraint upon the legislature, or at least upon the legislative members of the party. In communist legislatures, one-party domination coupled with the doctrine of "democratic centralism" meant that the legislative party was limited on all important matters by the central committee and its leadership external to the parliament. While no democratic party has either that practice or doctrine, the parliamentary–external conflict is always latent.

Summary

Both the party system and the internal party organization are important factors in establishing the autonomy and capability of the legislature. A one-party system permits executive domination of the legislature, while a highly fragmented party system debilitates the legislature, leaving it incapable of decision. A two-party system can also constrain a legislature through a disciplined and cohesive majority party. It is a "several"-party system that encourages more legislative autonomy (Mezey 1991).

The degree of the parties' internal organization is also an important factor in legislative autonomy. It is hard for the American congressional parties to form partywide views, and those parties have, in comparison with the European, a rudimentary structure of internal decision making. The British have collective party leadership through the cabinet and the opposition shadow cabinet, but otherwise also have a relatively undeveloped internal committee structure.

Some of the continental parliamentary parties have an elaborate structure of internal party committees, and a correspondingly regular-ized method of arriving at partywide policy decisions. It is these oppo-sition parties that not only oppose the government, but also can formulate alternative views. Even the members of the governing parties, if well organized, are able effectively to bargain with their own cabinet mem-bers to arrive at government policies that are acceptable to their party members in parliament. The combination of these two circumstances of party—system and internal organization—is an important element in legislative policy activism. If one party has a majority, as in Britain and the United States, and if both parties have a weak internal struc-ture, decision-making power will be found elsewhere. In Britain, deci-sions are made by the governing cabinet sustained by the party majority, but not by the party as a whole. In the U.S. Congress, the congressional committees are more the locus of legislative decisions.

4

Committees: The Internal Organization of Parliament, II

Lenin contemptuously dismissed parliaments as "mere talking shops." The specialized means by which legislatures work long and hard on substantive issues, the committees, were not well developed in Western Europe at the time of his comment. Forty years earlier, however, Woodrow Wilson noted that the committees were the workshop of the American Congress (Box 4.1). A more recent examination of committees in eight parliaments observed that "committees are the workhorses of legislatures" (Shaw 1979, 420).

This chapter considers both the activities and the structure of legislative committees and concludes with a review of attempted reforms of committees, considering throughout the interaction between parties and committees. We begin with a consideration of the two main types of committees found in democratic legislatures.

Types of Committees

The most active and effective committee systems among the world's democratic legislatures tend to have several characteristics. First, their jurisdiction is defined by subject matter, and that, in turn, tends to parallel the structure of the administrative agencies. Second, membership on the committees tends to be permanent for the duration of the legislative term between elections, and further, tends to last across a number of legislative terms. Third, chairmanships tend to go to the committee members of long experience on their committees.

Box 4.1

Talk and Work in Parliaments

Lenin, the revolutionary, on Western European parliaments and the newly created Duma, or legislature, in Russia, which he opposed:

"Parliament is given up to talk for the special purpose of fooling the 'common people' . . . mere talking shops."

State and Revolution (1917)
Quoted in Tucker 1975, 343

Wilson, the democrat, on the U.S. House of Representatives, of which he disapproved:

"It legislates in its committee-rooms. . . . Congress in session is Congress on public exhibition, whilst Congress in its committee-rooms is Congress at work."

Congressional Government (1885)
Quoted in Wilson 1956, 69

A system of permanent committees with durable membership provides the members with the essential resources of time, experience, and staff to become familiar with the substantive issues within the jurisdiction of the committee. They also become familiar with the administrative agencies and outside interest groups active on those issues. The senior members of a committee may very well have longer experience on the job than does the relevant minister. The senior leadership in the parliamentary committee system may be more experienced in office than is the Government of the Day. The parliaments of Sweden and Germany and the U.S. Congress have this type of committee system.

At the other extreme, the Westminster model, committees are not permanent (although the British term is "standing"; see appendix C), the members meet on an ad hoc basis for each bill, and the bill can be on any topic. Originally intended as smaller versions of the floor, the members sit by party on opposite sides of the room. The party groups are led, as they are on the floor, by the minister on the government side and by the opposition front bench spokesman on the other (Walkland 1979b, 252–64). These temporary ad hoc committees are "bill commit-

Table 4.1

Contrasting U.S. and British Committee Systems

Criteria	U.S. Congress	U.K. Commons
Jurisdiction	Fixed; parallel agencies	Single bill
Tenure	Permanent	Ad hoc; temporary
Chairmanship	Seniority on committee	Neutral; changing
Scope of activity	Legislation; administrative review; and investigations	Legislation
Place in stage of legislative procedure	Initial; prior to floor debate	Secondary; after floor approval
Discretion over bill	Complete	Details only
Bill version on floor	Committee	Government
Floor leaders in charge of bill	Committee	Government and party

tees," in that they work on legislative proposals. The contrasting features of these two types of legislative committees are summarized in Table 4.1.

Beginning in 1979, the British House of Commons instituted a new structure of departmental committees. They investigate and review the conduct of administration and the effectiveness of policy. They do not, however, work on legislation. They have the structural characteristics of the permanent committees discussed above, but they are excluded from the review of legislation. Currently, one reform under consideration in Britain is that these committees also examine proposed legislation. They are now a hybrid between the two main and polar types of committees (Hansard Society 1992; Jogerst 1993).

The two major types of committee systems—the permanent and the ad hoc—are capable of very different actions on legislation. In effect, the job of the Westminster model of ad hoc bill committees is to adopt the bill proposed by the government. The committee can consider amendments, and even adopts amendments if the minister in charge accepts them. The committee is severely limited by the previous action of the House in adopting a bill "in principle" on the floor, before sending the bill to committee (see appendix A). The task of the committee is limited to amendments of detail. The government uses the committee to protect the government's legislative program. If the cabinet has a majority in the House, and if the parties vote by party discipline, that objective is achieved at all stages, including the committee. "Parliament's role vis-à-vis the executive is reactive and supportive" at all stages (Drewry 1988, 131). Government control of bill committees reflects and is part of government control of the floor.

In the model of permanent legislative committees, however, the members have greater possibilities of amending proposed bills. American congressional committees not only amend government bills but also reject them, and initiate and adopt their own proposals. In the Swedish and German examples, the committees are the prime locale in which the experts of the several parties meet, and in which interparty negotiations occur. These negotiations are also a government–parliamentary negotiation, often resulting in significant changes to the government's draft legislation. In the German Bundestag, for example, of 339 laws passed in the 1976–80 period, 59 percent were amended in committee; that proportion rose to almost 66 percent in the 1983–87 term (Steffani 1990, 282). The extent of these legislative changes within the committees depends upon both the majority–minority composition of the cabinet and the internal decision-making structure of the parliamentary parties.

In a French variation, the permanent committees are required by the constitution to be few and large, and thus to have a broad and vague jurisdiction. They have, however, evolved a practical way of getting work done: they form smaller working groups on specific bills, which also permits opposition members active responsibility on legislation (Ehrmann and Schain 1992, 333).

Activities and Tasks

Committees may undertake a wide variety of tasks within the legislature. Parliaments vary not only in the structural types of committees, discussed above, but in the distribution of functions among specific committees. The long list of possible activities includes legislation, administrative review, investigations, and appropriations (Shaw 1979, 370–77).

Legislation

As indicated above, the permanent committees that parallel the structure of the ministries have the greatest possibility for independent thought and action on legislation. At one extreme—the U.S. model—the committees themselves often initiate legislation. In the Westminster model, at the other extreme, the task of the ad hoc bill committee is to protect the government's bill. In the European continental parliaments, the permanent committees' latitude of action depends upon the party system, but their permanent structure gives them the possibility of independent action.

Administrative Review

Committees that parallel the structure of the ministries have the capability of reviewing and evaluating the conduct of administration by specific ministries. This capability was the intention of the 1979 creation in Britain of their departmental review committees, and, to a considerable degree, has been achieved (Box 4.2). Such committees may also investigate policy problems within the jurisdiction of the department and the committee. Within most legislatures, one or more committees are likely to have administrative review as their main purpose. The Committee on Public Accounts in Britain (Bates 1988, 187–93) and the Government Operations Committee in both houses of the U.S. Congress are examples.

Investigations

Committees can investigate major public policy issues or allegations of scandal and official impropriety. Perhaps the "Watergate" committee of the U.S. Senate during the Nixon administration is one of the best known throughout the world. More recently, issues of public health in dairy products, and banking scandals have been the objects of investigations by the British departmental committees. The Industry and Trade Committee, for example, held hearings on military exports to Iraq (Box 4.3). The "tangled tale of Westland" is another British example, investigated by three of the departmental committees, which, however, resulted in an "evasive reply" from the government (Drewry 1989d, 411–16). In the United States, Senator Fulbright, as chairman

---

Box 4.2

**British Departmental Committees and Administration:
Two-Way Interaction**

"It is a feature of the select committee system that both civil servants
and ministers appear before them. . . . The ability of committees which
are permanent and control their own agenda to return to topics over
several parliamentary sessions is the notable feature. . . . That, coupled
with their near comprehensive coverage of departments, has
significantly increased the accountability of the administration . . .

"Examination takes place on the record, and (usually) in public. . . . What
might therefore pass unchallenged on the floor of the House is not so
likely to slip through an alert select committee. . . . It is also an
opportunity for officials and ministers to put on record a reasoned
version of the government's view and dispose of comments from critics."

Giddings 1989, 376–77

---

of the Senate Committee on Foreign Relations, held a long and detailed series of hearings on U.S. policy in the Far East. Held during the
Vietnam War, the hearings had an important effect on U.S. foreign
policy in the succeeding decade.

Appropriations

If committees are the locale in which serious work is done, how should
the task of reviewing and approving the government's requested appropriations be allocated to the committees? There are two main an-
swers to this question. One, illustrated by the U.S. Congress, is a
specialized committee. The second and more common solution is to
allocate the appropriations for each department or purpose to each of
the subject matter committees, and then to give major coordinating
responsibility to a single committee to bring the bill to the floor (Peters
1991, 82–84). There is still a third solution—the British—largely to
ignore the appropriations task. The Treasury and Civil Service Committee (one of the departmental review committees) does review the
major outlines of the intended budget. Otherwise, the government's

Box 4.3

 TRADE AND INDUSTRY COMMITTEE

COMMITTEE OFFICE   HOUSE OF COMMONS   LONDON SW1A 0AA

──────── Telephone 071-219 5469/5776/5777/5779 ────────

PRESS NOTICE

TAKEOVERS AND MERGERS

The Committee's report on takeovers and mergers will be published as the First Report 1991-92 HC 90 on **Thursday 19 December**. A press conference will be held in Committee Room 15 at the House of Commons at 1030.

Advance copies of the Report will be sent to all those who submitted written or gave oral evidence on **Tuesday 17 December**. Copies will be placed in the Press Gallery, House of Commons on Tuesday 17 December at 1030. Other <u>journalists</u> who wish to receive an advance copy should register their interest with the Committee staff (071 219 5777/5779).

INVESTOR PROTECTION

The Committee will take oral evidence from Sir David Walker, Chairman of the Securities and Investments Board, on Wednesday 18 December at 1030 in Committee Room 15 at the House of Commons. The principal subject will be the 1990-91 annual report of SIB, but a wide range of investor protection issues may be raised.

The Committee has received more than twenty memoranda from interested parties. The oral and written evidence will be published in late January or early February.

The Committee has no current plans to hold other oral evidence sessions on this subject or to produce a report.

EXPORTS TO IRAQ

The Committee's programme of evidence sessions is as follows:

Wed. 15 January	1030: Oral evidence from Dr Christopher Cowley
	1630: Oral evidence from Dr Cowley (continued - if necessary)
Tues. 21 January	1030: Further oral evidence from Walter Somers
Wed. 22 January	1030: Oral evidence from MOD
Wed. 29 January	1030: Oral evidence from Customs & Excise

Other meetings will be arranged.

The oral evidence taken on 26 November from DTI officials and on 3 and 4 December by Eagle Trust, Walter Somers and Sheffield Forgemasters will be published in January 1992.

TRADE WITH HONG KONG AND THE CHINESE HINTERLAND

The Committee has decided to conduct a short inquiry into "future UK trade prospects with Hong Kong, the Chinese hinterland and adjacent markets".

Written evidence is being sought from interested parties, but the Committee is willing to consider any evidence received. (Anyone wishing to submit evidence should contact the Clerks of the Committee).

Oral evidence sessions are planned to start on Tuesday 4 February. The Committee intends to visit the area in early March. It hopes to publish a report by the end of the parliamentary session.

NOTE FOR EDITORS

The Committee is appointed under Standing Order No. 130 of the House of Commons to examine the expenditure, administration and policy of the Department of Trade and Industry and associated public bodies, and similar matters within the responsibilities of the Secretary of State for Northern Ireland. It has the power to send for persons, papers and records.

The Members of the Committee are:

Mr Kenneth Warren MP (Chairman)	Con, Hastings & Rye
Mr Menzies Campbell MP	LibDem, Fife North East
Mr Jim Cousins MP	Lab, Newcastle upon Tyne Central
Mr James Cran MP	Con, Beverley
Mr Stan Crowther MP	Lab, Rotherham
Rt Hon Dr John Gilbert MP	Lab, Dudley East
Sir Anthony Grant MP	Con, Cambridgeshire South West
Dr Keith Hampson MP	Con, Leeds North West
Mr Doug Hoyle MP	**Lab, Warrington North**
Mr Robin Maxwell-Hyslop MP	Con, Tiverton
Mr Barry Porter MP	Con, Wirral South

For inquiries please telephone 071 219 5779/5777

12 December 1991

requests are routinely approved by Parliament (Robinson 1988).

Appropriations are a serious and intense task. Budgets are long and detailed documents. Each of the U.S. Appropriations Committees themselves, one in each chamber, is a minicommittee system, referring each of the thirteen major portions of the expenditure budget to a separate subcommittee. The subcommittees tend to parallel the structure of the administrative agencies, and thus of the whole congressional committee system itself. Since expenditure review tends to be a year-long task in Congress, a set of subcommittees with this specialized task is the result (Franklin 1992). The German Appropriations Committee has a similar internal structure of subcommittees (Schwarz and Shaw 1976, 282–83).

In most democracies, however, the legislature makes far fewer independent and specific decisions about expenditures than does the U.S. Congress, and spends far less time on that matter. Thus, the tasks of expenditure review and approval can be less of a time-consuming task for them and their committees than they are in the United States. Furthermore, some legislatures are prohibited from either increasing expenditures or reducing revenues without the consent of the government. In Germany, government control through the Budget Committee is the effective means of enforcing this rule (Steffani 1990, 282–83).

Members and Officers

In most parliaments, the members of committees and their presiding officers are selected through the parliamentary parties. How the parties accomplish this task, however, varies greatly among the worlds' legislatures.

In most countries, committee memberships are allocated proportionally to the size of the parties in parliament. A majority party or coalition of parties is thus assured of a majority of committee assignments. There are arguments at times whether this usual formula means that every committee should be proportional to the chamber in party composition. For small parties, and fairly small committees, the mathematics are difficult to work out exactly.

In the Swedish Riksdag, for example, at one time the small Communist Party demanded a seat on every committee, which would have increased its share of the total number of committee seats above its proportion in the whole chamber. Because the Social Democrats needed the Communists' support to continue in government, the Social Democrats relinquished some of their committee seats to the Communists.

This solution illustrates the many different and informal ways practical politicians have of developing pragmatic solutions to difficult questions. This particular dispute was debated on the floor, but the solution was developed through private discussions among party leaders. Party ratios on committees are a vital matter to parties, and thus the solutions are developed through negotiation among the party leaders. Committees are officially the creatures of the chamber; their existence and composition are decided by parties.

A far more serious question than seat ratios is the party distribution of committee chairmanships. In part, the solution varies with the party system: it is simple in two-party systems, but complex in multiparty systems.

In the British and American two-party systems, the majority party holds the chairmanships of most if not all committees. In the U.S. Congress, the majority holds all committee and subcommittee chairmanships. In the British House of Commons, the majority party chairs most departmental review committees. The long-standing Public Accounts Committee, reviewing the financial performance of government, has a particularly important audit function, and thus the chairmanship is allocated to the opposition party (Bates 1988, 187–93). Party control over the newer departmental committees has been lessened in that the members are selected by a committee of selection, rather than by the party whips (Drewry 1989c; Johnson 1988, 158). In the United States, occasionally special investigative committees will have co-chairs, as do the ethics committees, one for each of the two parties.

In multiparty systems in Europe, committee offices are usually allocated proportionally among all of the larger parties. In Sweden, for example, the small Communist and Green parties never held a committee chairmanship. If committees have a vice-chairmanship, that position is also distributed among the parties. To use another Swedish example, when the seats have been almost evenly distributed between the two major coalitions, each committee had a chairman from one of the party coalitions and a vice-chairman from the other (Olson et al. 1983).

The allocation of committee memberships and offices among the parties is usually officially made by the whole membership on the floor, but is arranged in advance through interparty negotiation. One indicator of a democratic parliament in its beginning stages, as in Central Europe, is that these party-managed functions are not always understood by or acceptable to all of the new members. This committee personnel function is one of the chamber management tasks customarily arranged by parties, and illustrates their cooperative antagonist relationship in making parliaments function.

Committees, Parties, and Legislation on the Floor

Membership on the chamber committees is closely related to the membership and structure of the parties' own internal committees discussed in chapter 3. The members of a party committee on, for example, agriculture, are also the members from that party on the chamber committee on agriculture. The chamber committee is a meeting place for the experts from all of the parties on agriculture. The chamber committees are thus able to be the forum within which multiparty agreements can be negotiated.

Committees are also an important means by which the government cabinet, through its supporting party members, can negotiate with other parties to identify likely sources of disagreement and also of agreement on proposed policies. Many of these discussions are private and informal. One committee chairman in a continental parliament, for example, pointed to the sofa in his office as the place where the leader of another party sat, who was a member of his committee, when the two of them arrived at an agreement on how the committee would act on a government proposal (interview).

In most parliaments, committees lead debate and voting on the floor. In some countries, the committee's chairperson brings the bill to the floor, with the other leaders of the other parties on his or her committee leading their respective party groups in floor debate. In other countries, such as France and the Czech Republic, bills are presented to the chamber by "rapporteurs" who are members of the committee with particular responsibility for the bill under consideration.

One measure of the reduced importance of bill committees in the British Parliament is that floor debate is led by the minister and the opposition front bench spokesperson, when a bill comes from committee to the floor. Their floor leadership illustrates and is a rationale for the dominance of these same government and party officials within the bill committee itself.

The debates, and especially the voting alignment, within the committee usually predict the final vote on the floor. This result is particularly characteristic of parliaments with party discipline—which is found in most of the world, with the notable exception of the United States. Even there, the distribution of the committee members on the bill as a whole and on major points of dispute is usually predictive of how most members will vote at the floor stage.

Because of the central place of committees in most democratic legislatures, government ministers sometimes pay close attention to the officers and members of the committees. A government cabinet with majority support, and with party discipline, can afford to neglect the committees. In multiparty legislatures, however, or in the U.S. Congress with party-free voting, cabinet ministers have many reasons to know and to meet with the committee, not only as a whole, but also with individual members and in small groups. Not infrequently, cabinet "secretaries" (the American term) complain that they spend half their time "on the Hill," mostly with the committees holding jurisdiction over portions of their departments. Committee members, too, often are invited to meetings, meals, and parties, in the offices and homes of the cabinet members (Cronin 1980, 258–59). In many parliaments, government ministers meet with and participate in committee meetings, whether or not they themselves remain formal members of parliament.

There is usually much less party discipline in committees than on the floor (Shaw 1979, 422–26). Parties usually require disciplined voting when a bill comes to the floor. For this reason, the relatively well developed committee system in the Polish Sejm under Communist rule was the place within which members could, and increasingly did, amend and even block the government's proposals. For the same reason, committees that consider bills before the floor stage, as in Germany, Sweden, and the United States, have greater latitude of thought and action than do Westminster bill committees, which consider legislation only after its acceptance by second reading debate (Shaw 1979, 417).

Committee Documents

The documents produced by committees are among the most important of all materials published by the legislature. Most committees produce a written statement to the chamber on a bill. That document might be the text of the bill as recommended by the committee. In Sweden and the United States, the committee "report" is often a thick document that explains in detail the views of the committee as a whole and of specific members. These reports also often indicate the history of the committee's consideration of the bill.

The pattern of members' names attached to the report signals the party and/or factional alignment on the bill in question. In the United States Congress, there is often both a majority and a minority report. In addition, a small number of members, or even individual members, may append additional or "supplemental" statements expressing their hopes and fears about the bill as a whole or about specific portions of the bill. This practice is a growing one in Sweden, although the party majority that is formed in committee is sustained on the floor (Arter 1990, 133–34).

The American and Canadian committees hold public "hearings" in which witnesses from the ministry, from interest groups, and from regional and local governments present their views on the question before the committee, and respond to questions from committee members. These "hearings" are published and become a vital part of the legislative history of the bill or issue under consideration. Since the committee hearings can last from a half hour to twenty or more days, the thickness of the resulting published transcript of the proceedings also varies greatly. Most parliaments, however, do not hold public "hearings."

Since the ad hoc legislative committees on the British model do not hold public hearings, this printed documentary record does not exist for them. But the British departmental review committees do hold public hearings and do issue reports. Their hearings record, "Proceedings," and their final recommendations, "Report," are important sources of information. Thus, in Britain, there is a lack of a thorough documentary record on legislation, but there is a more complete record on the Commons' investigation of selected issues and of administrative activity. Titles of committee documents, as illustrations of what is typically published in each legislature, are included in Box 4.4.

Committees, as units of the legislature, conduct at least some of their activity in public view, and the extensive set of documents is an expression of their public accessibility. The parliamentary parties, by contrast, are entirely private. They meet and act in secret, and many of their documents are "internal" only for the party members. Even the

Box 4.4

Committee Documents by Country and Type

I. U.S. Congress
Type A. Hearings
Chamber: House of Representatives
Committee/subcommittee: Committee on Banking, Finance, and Urban Affairs; Subcommittee on Economic Stabilization
Title: Industrial Competitiveness Act: Hearings on HR 4360
Date: Nov. 16, 1983–Feb. 2, 1984
Doc. #: Serial no. 98–79 (Committee hearing no. 79 in 98th Congress)
Type B. Report
Chamber: House of Representatives
Committee: Committee on Banking, Finance, and Urban Affairs
Title: Industrial Competitiveness Act (HR 4360)
Date: 1984
Doc. #: Report 98–697, Part I (Committee report no. 697 of the 98th Congress, Part I of a two-part report. Part II came from a different committee)

II. British Parliament
Type: Hearings and Report
Chamber: House of Commons
Committee: Trade and Industry Committee
Title: The Operation of the Export Credits Guarantee Department Together with the proceedings of the Committee relating to the Report, the Minutes of Evidence and Appendices
Date: January 23, 1985
Doc. #: Session 1984–85, First Report (first report of this committee during the 1984–85 year)

III. Swedish Riksdag
Type: Report
Committee: Naeringsutskottet (Business Affairs Committee)
Title: Naeringsutskottets betaenkande om utrikeshandel (Business Affairs Committee Report on Foreign Trade)
Date: April 14, 1988
Doc. #: NU1987/88:28 (Document no. 28 from the NU, [Naeringsutskottet] Business Affairs Committee in the 1987–88 year)

IV. Canadian Parliament
Type: Report
Chamber: House of Commons
Committee: Standing Committee on External Affairs and International Trade
Title: The Canada–United States Free Trade Agreement
Date: October 5, 1987
Doc. #: Issue no. 66

whip notice is secret in some parliaments. Most committees, however, deliberate on legislation in private; the "markup" sessions of American committees did not become open to the public until the 1970s, for example.

Coordination

The more important and active the committees, the greater the organizational problems they create. One source of difficulty is in the definition of committee jurisdiction. Often, society's major problems, and especially the newer ones, cut across the jurisdiction of several committees. Another organizational difficulty is presented in bicameral legislatures.

Committee Coordination

One way to coordinate several committees is to divide a long and complex bill into as many parts as there are relevant committees, a typical U.S. congressional practice. Another is to form a joint subcommittee among the several committees, a Polish practice. A third solution is to permit several committees to report their recommendations to one main committee, a Swedish solution.

A one-time experiment in the U.S. House was the creation of a special committee to handle the massive energy bill during the Carter administration. That committee, composed of the leaders of the standing committees holding legislative jurisdiction, had both policy and schedule coordination functions.

Several committees must be coordinated on most bills in the Central European new democracies. For example, each Committee on Law and Legislation has a key supervision function on a wide range of bills that also belong to other more topically defined committees.

Chamber Coordination

Bicameral parliaments face the task of arriving at a single version of a bill if the two chambers disagree. Typically, the Westminster type of parliament does not involve the committees in this matter, but many other legislatures do. Germany, for example, has a special interchamber Mediation Committee (Steffani 1990, 277–78).

The U.S. Congress forms bill-specific "conference committees," with the members coming from the chamber committees holding major jurisdiction over the bill. In effect, the chair and senior members of the chamber committees are the leading members of the conference committee. Since the two chambers may have different majority parties, as in the 1980s, a conference committee may not only be an interchamber committee, but also an interparty negotiation committee. Exactly the same dynamic occurred in Germany in the early 1990s, when Christian Democrats were the governing party in the Bundestag, while Social Democrats gained the majority in the Bundesrat or upper chamber.

The New and the Old

Committee systems, like all other features of legislatures, are subject to change. Strong committee systems lead to dissatisfaction because either they do not correspond to the changing agenda of public issues, or they are organizationally cumbersome. Legislatures with weak committees attempt to create strong ones. In either case, there are constant efforts to revise and to "reform" the existing committee system.

The most important reorganization of congressional committees in the United States occurred in the 1946 Legislative Reorganization Act, which reduced the over fifty committees per chamber to a more manageable number of approximately twenty. Their jurisdictions were correspondingly revised, by becoming broader in scope. That reorganization has lasted until the present day, though not without revisions in the 1970s (Smith and Deering 1984, 22–55).

One important change in the United States has been the increased number and importance of subcommittees. Now all committees have several subcommittees, and they are the ones that hold the hearings, issue the report, and lead debate on the floor. Sometimes, the full committee and subcommittee are in conflict over a bill, so that negotiation within the committee can be difficult and protracted (Smith and Deering 1984, 125–66).

The lack of permanent committees, and MP dissatisfaction with their own lack of power, led to the creation of departmental committees in the British Commons in 1979. The Canadian House had been experimenting with similar reforms earlier, and in the 1980s again attempted to strengthen their committees (Franks 1987, 161–85; Jogerst 1993).

In both Britain and Canada, there has been a long period of experi-mentation and learning. British ministers now have the experience of being subjected to probing questions from their colleagues and sup-posed equals, the noncabinet MPs. MPs themselves had to learn how to obtain the cooperation of and information from the ministers. Civil servants were also subjected to questioning, and they, too, had to learn. In both countries, the new committee structure gave wide scope to the chairpersons: their personalities and their vision of how the committees might function led to considerable differences in how each committee acted and in the impact each committee had on the affairs of the House (Drewry 1989b, 359–60; 1989d, 405–06).

Change and reinvigoration can come from other sources, too. In Sweden, for example, the Social Democratic members of Riksdagen had long become accustomed to accepting the policies of their own government. When, for the first time in the personal experience of the members, they became the opposition in 1979, they learned the plea-sures of disagreement. One Social Democratic committee chair, during a subsequent Social Democratic government, commented that never again would his party in parliament passively accept what his own government might propose (interview). He was, as chairman, in a posi-tion to act on his views, at least on those matters within the jurisdiction of his committee. He was also, in his dual role as leader of his own party's committee on the same topic, able to act on his views within the governmental party itself.

Summary

The many varieties of committees in the world's democratic parlia-ments may be reduced to two major types: permanent committees, which parallel the structure of administrative agencies, and temporary committees with a limited purpose. The Westminster model illustrates the latter, while the U.S. Congress and the German Bundestag illustrate the former.

The British and the Canadians have introduced important innova-tions in their committee systems, greatly complicating this simple two-fold typology. The British have retained the ad hoc committee system for legislation, while adding a departmentally related structure of com-mittees to review policy questions and to investigate the conduct of the administration. The Canadians have gone further, now referring legis-lation to departmentally related committees.

In general, it is the permanent committees, which possess permanent legislative jurisdiction and parallel the structure of administrative agencies, that have the greater capacity for independent thought and action on policy questions. As control by a single party declines, as in the U.S. Congress through a lack of party discipline, or as in Scandinavia through coalition and minority governments, the opportunity increases for committee independence. It is the skill of the committee chairs as individuals and the accumulated experience of the whole committee that equip it to act with expertise, independently of the executive, in the circumstances of reduced party control in the parliament.

5

Legislative–Executive Relations

In considering the relationship between the legislature and the executive, the confusion, at least in the English language, between the terms "legislature" and "parliament" is at its greatest. The two terms imply very different relationships. Since the legislative/parliamentary interaction with the executive is the single most important relationship in the policy process of democracies, the terminological confusion is all the greater and more important.

The key question for legislatures concerns their independence from the executive. To what extent can a legislature act independently of the chief executive on legislation, or on constituency problems, or on any other matter? Do legislatures agree to executive proposed legislation? Can they, and do they, disagree? To what extent do legislatures initiate their own policy proposals?

This chapter reviews several elements together. We begin with the chief executive, and also consider the cabinet and the administrative departments. The chief executive is usually termed prime minister in parliaments in the Westminster model, or premier in French-speaking countries, while the chief executive in dual-branch structures is termed president.

Constitutional Design and Chief Executives

Among democratic political systems, the distinction between the parliamentary system of Britain and a separation of powers system in the United States illustrates the two opposite ways in which democracies have structured the relationship between the executive and legislative authorities of government (Figure 5.1).

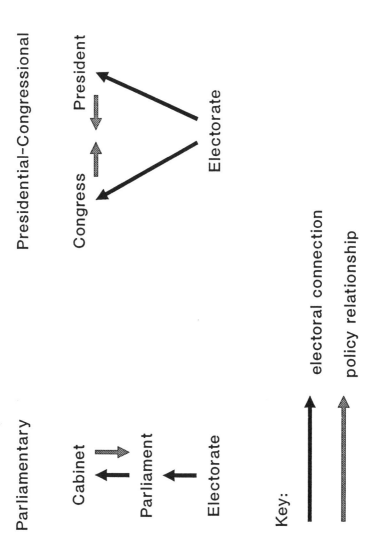

Figure 5.1. **Parliamentary and Presidential-Congressional Systems**

Parliamentary

Presidential-Congressional

Cabinet

Parliament

Electorate

President

Congress

Electorate

Key:

electoral connection

policy relationship

Dual-Branch and Unitary Designs

From these two very different constitutional designs flows an important difference: the two sets of offices in a dual-branch structure are occupied by different persons, while in a parliamentary or unitary system, they are occupied by the same persons. In the United States, a member of Congress may be appointed to a cabinet position, but he or she must then resign his or her congressional seat. When Senator John F. Kennedy became President Kennedy, he was required to resign from the Senate. When President Clinton appointed Senator Lloyd Bentsen as secretary of the treasury in 1993, Bentsen was required to resign from the Senate. In Britain, the opposite is true: the prime minister is a member of the House of Commons, and all cabinet members are, or become, members of either the Commons or the House of Lords.

An important practical consequence follows for the leadership of the legislature from the two different constitutional systems. The British Parliament is led by the Government of the Day, the ministers of the Crown, while in the United States, Congress is led by persons who are not part of the presidential administration or his cabinet. There may be close personal and political relations between the president and individual members of Congress, but there is no appointive or salaried relationship. In Britain, about a third of the members of the majority party hold appointive governmental positions, and thus receive an increased salary. In the United States no representative or senator is on the "government payroll" in the same fashion.

In the British parliamentary system, the government controls both the agenda and the final decisions of Parliament. It does so through its party majority. The cabinet sets the schedule, and decides which bills will occupy the time of Parliament. The cabinet minister in charge of a bill will lead Commons debate through all stages, from the opening "first" and "second" readings, through the committee, and back on the floor for final debate and voting. (For a description of these legislative steps, see appendix A.)

In the United States, cabinet members may be as concerned with a congressional bill as a British cabinet minister might be, but they are nowhere to be seen on the floor. There is no place for them to sit; and were they to appear on the floor in an official capacity, there would be a constitutional crisis. Instead, a cabinet member, or staff persons from the White House, may be in the gallery with other visitors, or may be in a room near the chamber floor. They may have very strong views on the bill under consideration, but their views must be expressed, if they are to be expressed on the floor at all, by senators and representatives who have accepted the responsibility of leadership on that particular bill. Senator Robert Dole as Republican leader and Senator George Mitchell as Democratic leader often speak for their respective presidents on the floor, for no president may speak for himself in that place.

A very practical consequence of this distinction for the whole legislative body, and also for individual members, is that the vote on legislation has a completely different meaning in the two systems. In the British system, any vote can be interpreted as a "vote of no confidence," deciding the tenure in office of the government cabinet. In the U.S. system, no vote in Congress has that significance.

For example, in July 1993, a hardy band of Conservative "Eurosceptics" voted against their prime minister on the ratification of the Maastricht Treaty of the European Common Market. Prime Minister Major immediately called for a vote of no-confidence the very next day. All of the party "rebels" on the day previous then voted in support of the prime minister on the vote of no confidence. They thereby kept Mr. Major in office and themselves in the Conservative Party (Box 5.1).

One Tory MP was apparently on vacation in Bermuda. The member who represented the Torbay constituency was promptly dubbed the Member for Bermuda-North, and there was speculation that the Conservative whip would be withdrawn from him for having not voted in support of the prime minister on the no-confidence motion. Withdrawal of the whip would mean both expulsion from the parliamentary party and denial of his party's renomination at the next election (*Financial Times* July 24, 1993; Norton 1993).

The government in a parliamentary system must control the votes of its parliamentary members, while the president does not need to try to exercise that control to stay in office. He stays in office whether or not Congress votes the way he wants. No British MP can afford to vote against his party on such a question; in the U.S. Congress, that question never arises.

Paradoxically, the very system intended to ensure parliament's control over the executive has led to exactly the opposite flow of control. While the dual-branch system is often praised because it provides for a

Box 5.1

With Friends like These . . . ?

From the news report:

"Mr John Major's threat of a general election yesterday pulled the Conservative party back from the brink of self-destruction. . . . With Tory Eurosceptics threatening revenge after being forced to abandon their rebellion and ministers acknowledging that Mr. Major's authority had suffered another blow, there was speculation about a leadership challenge in the autumn."

From the editorial:

"In the end the power of a prime minister is the power of dissolution. By making the Tory rebels choose between the Masstricht treaty and the likely extinction not just of the government, but perhaps of their party, Mr Major has played for the highest possible stakes and won. . . . By turning the question into one of confidence . . . the political price he (the Prime Minister) has had to pay is a steep one. Many in his party are embittered . . . although he will be encouraged that none pushed rebellion to the point of losing the whip and so further reducing his majority."

Financial Times, July 24, 1993

stable executive, it also permits the legislature to be, or to become, independent of the executive (see Box 5.2).

Variations in Constitutional Design

The United States and Britain exemplify the two opposite ways developed by democracies to structure the legislative-executive relationship. The continental European democracies have developed variations between these two extremes (Lijphart 1984, 70). In Germany, the cabinet sits in the Bundestag, not as party leaders on the floor, but on benches in the front, facing the whole parliament. In Sweden, cabinet members resign their Riksdag seats, in favor of party "alternates" who take their place. As cabinet members, they sit to the side of the chamber and participate in floor exchanges. But they do not vote, for they themselves are no longer members.

These varied seating arrangements in turn signal a political differen-

---

Box 5.2

Who Worries? From the Prime Minister to the President

Prime Minister Winston Churchill to President Franklin Roosevelt, during World War II:

"You, Mr. President, are concerned to what extent you can act without the approval of Congress. You don't worry about your cabinet. On the other hand, I never worry about parliament, but I continuously have to consult and have the support of my cabinet."

Quoted in Schlesinger 1992

---

tiation between "the Government" and "the Parliament," in which the continental parliaments do not always agree with the policy views of the governing cabinet that they have created and could also dismiss. This distinction is also felt within the government party, between those who have become ministers and those who remain legislators.

There are numerous variations on the constitutional designs of the relationship between legislature and executive, with two prominent types termed "premier-president" and "president-parliamentary" (Shugart and Carey 1992). Variations within presidential or dual-branch systems are found in Finland and France (Blondel 1990; Lijphart 1984, 83–84).

Party System and Government Selection

In parliamentary systems, the configuration of party strength in the legislature is the determining factor in both the selection and retention of the prime minister and the cabinet. In dual-branch systems, however, party strength in the legislature is ordinarily irrelevant to the election of the president.

In the U.S. dual-branch system and in the French variant, the selection of the officers of the legislature itself is a function of the party system. Furthermore, the amount of support the legislature provides to the chief executive's proposals is also affected by the party composition of the legislature.

As the cases of both France and the United States illustrate, it is entirely possible to have a chief executive of one party, with the legislature controlled by another. In France, they cooperate through "cohabitation." When the National Assembly has had a party majority differing from the president, the president has even shared executive authority with a premier, whom he has appointed, from that different party majority (Poulard 1990).

In the United States, divided party control has become normal, or at least frequent. Ever since the 1954 midterm congressional election, Democrats have held a majority in the House of Representatives, and also for most of that time, in the Senate. Republicans, however, have held the White House for most of that same period. Split-party control increases the independence of Congress from the president and increases the opportunity for each branch to criticize the other.

Very infrequently does a British prime minister lose a vote of no confidence. By a one-vote margin, Labour Prime Minister James Callaghan lost a no-confidence vote in 1979; he promptly resigned, and called for new elections. A few weeks later, Conservatives won a majority of seats and Margaret Thatcher, the Conservative parliamentary leader, became prime minister.

The party configuration in the 1979 British vote was unusual, in that Labour had lost a majority of seats. Though the largest party in the House, it was only a plurality, not a majority, party, with several smaller parties holding the balance of power. Usually the British prime minister, as a consequence of the two-party system, has a party majority and thus always survives a vote of no confidence, as did Prime Minister Major in 1993. In 1979, however, the British had something more complicated than a simple two-party configuration in the House of Commons.

The prospect of losing a vote of no confidence directly leads to an emphasis upon party discipline. In the Canadian practice of the Westminster model, every vote is considered a "confidence" vote, leading to considerable frustration among the members. A suggested reform in Canada, as noted earlier, has been to differentiate "confidence" votes from less critical issues, thus freeing members to vote more individually. Leaders of neither party have been very receptive to that suggestion.

At about the same time that Prime Minister Major narrowly survived a vote of no confidence, his opposite number in Japan narrowly lost his. The Liberal Democratic Party, in power for virtually all of the post–World War II period, divided, with sufficient members forming new factions who then voted against the prime minister, to cause his

---

Box 5.3

Japan's Liberal Democratic Party Factionalism

"The outcome of a no-confidence vote will hinge on . . . a pro-reform
LDP faction. . . . [If] the members of . . . [the] faction . . . [abstain], the
LDP will still have a small majority in the lower house, but if they vote
against the party, the . . . cabinet will fall. [The Premier's] advisers were
attempting to reach a compromise with LDP reformers last night, fearing
that the party would be badly bruised in a snap election."

Financial Times, June 17, 1993

---

defeat. A new election was held within a few weeks, the result of
which was a seven-party coalition agreeing to form a majority against
the LDP. A leader of one of the secessionist LDP factions, who had
formed his own new party, became that coalition's candidate for prime
minister (Box 5.3). This Japanese example shows the perils faced in
parliamentary systems by defections from within the prime minister's
own party (*Financial Times* June 17, 1993; *New York Times* June 19,
1993).

The frequent instability of governing cabinets in continental Europe,
and especially the experience of the Weimar Republic in the 1920s, led
Germany after World War II to devise a new "constructive vote of no
confidence." The Bundestag could vote down a government only if it
would, by the same vote, accept a replacement chancellor. This type of
vote has been used infrequently, for the party fragmentation it was
designed to ameliorate has not occurred.

Yet numerous cabinets of continental European democracies have
been either coalitions, or minorities, or even both. The stable German
governments have usually been coalitions between one of the two largest parties, CDU/CSU or SPD, with the perpetually smaller Free Democratic Party (FPD). They have entered into the coalition to provide
majority support to the cabinet (see Table 3.2). To provide a stable
majority base for the cabinet, Swedish Social Democrats have cooper-
ated with the much smaller Communist Party, though in neither that
nor any other Western European democracy have Communists been
permitted to enter the cabinet during the Cold War (with one short-
term exception in France).

Other coalition governments have been both superlarge and minority in size. At one time, Germany had a "grand coalition" in which both large parties joined in the government along with the much smaller party. Other examples of grand or at least oversized coalitions include Finland, Sweden, the Netherlands, and Israel (Lijphart 1984, 82–83; Steiner 1991, 122–26).

Minority governments have increased in frequency over the past decade, especially in Scandinavia (Steiner 1991, 126–29). There have been intense negotiations between the governing coalition on one side, and any one or combination of noncabinet parties on the other, to form a majority on behalf of any given bill or measure. Although the majority in parliament have not joined the governing cabinet, neither have they been willing or able to depose that minority government to replace it with a more acceptable substitute. The British phrase for a parliament without a single majority party is "hung" parliament, indicating both the rarity and disrepute of that circumstance in the United Kingdom. But in many European democracies, the lack of a single majority party is a normal fact of political life (Arter 1990, 132; Damgaard 1992, 192–94).

By and large, the stability of a governing cabinet, that is, its duration in office, varies with the party system. The more fragmented the party system in parliament, the shorter the cabinet's duration in office. Of course, the same circumstance makes the initial negotiations to form a government more difficult as well (Lijphart 1984, 125–26).

Selection of Candidates for Chief Executive

A potentially important source of variation among parliamentary systems is the different ways in which party leaders, that is, candidates for prime minister, are selected. In the British "parliamentary system" prototype, the party leader is selected by the parliamentary members of the party, who usually select from among their experienced leaders. In chapter 3, we saw how that method both selected and deselected Mrs. Thatcher as Conservative leader and prime minister.

Canada, Germany, and Israel, however, use an external selection system. They use party conventions, similar to an American presidential nominating convention, that select the party's candidate for prime minister. That person is not necessarily a member of parliament at the time of his or her selection. Because he or she must lead the party from inside parliament, however, he or she then runs for and is elected to a parliamentary seat. The German chancellor candidates often have been leaders in their *Land* or provincial parties, and have often been members of the Bundesrat as a consequence of having served as minister-president of their *Land* governments.

The 1992 Israeli election illustrates another characteristic of leadership selection: the three rivals for leadership of the then-ruling Likud party were all members, not only of the Knesset, but also of the cabinet, and two of them were challengers to the incumbent party leader and prime minister, Yitzhak Shamir. Their intraparty dispute was resolved, not by the party in the Knesset, but by a party convention outside of Parliament.

For the same 1992 election, the Israeli Labour Party adopted a new selection system. All party members in the electorate were eligible to vote to select the party's candidate for prime minister. The result was the selection of a rival (Yitzhak Rabin) who became prime minister, to the incumbent party leader (Shimon Peres), who then became foreign minister. The German SPD in 1993 adopted a similar leadership selection method, in which the minister-president of a *Land* was elected as the new party leader. These parties are moving toward the U.S. practice of a party primary. One attribute of the British method of party leadership selection is that the candidates have all served many years in Parliament. They know Parliament, they have served in lower cabinet positions, and they know each other. This "apprenticeship" method selects experienced persons as leaders (Rose 1991, 104–14). The Canadian and German methods, however, of external selection of party leaders do not always select persons with extensive parliamentary experience. The national convention of the Canadian Progressive Conservative Party in 1993, for example, did elect as its leader Kim Campbell, a person who had served in two previous cabinet posts, but who had been in Parliament for only five years (*New York Times* June 14, 1993).

Working Relationships: Legislation

Although constitutional designs differ in structuring the relationship between executive and legislature, there is, in practice, an intensive daily interchange, varying by both topic and function. Their exchanges mainly involve: legislation, budgets, the conduct of administration, the

Table 5.1

Bills in the German Bundestag, by Source

Source	Introduced		Passed		Passed as % Introduced
	N	%	N	%	
Government	3,685	60.50	3,120	78.53	84.67
Bundestag	2,053	33.71	736	18.53	35.85
Bundesrat	353	5.80	117	2.94	33.14
Total	6,091	100.00	3,973	100.00	

Source: Thaysen et al. (1990), Appendix A, Table 12.
Note: Totals and percentages differ from source. Years included: 1949–87.

selection of governmental personnel, and debates upon current topics. This section examines the parliament–government working relationship on legislation.

Government Bills and Private Member Bills

In most democratic legislatures, the practice approaches a "90 percent rule": the cabinet proposes at least 90 percent of the legislative agenda, and at least 90 percent of what it proposes is adopted (Loewenberg and Patterson 1979, 267; Schwarz and Shaw 1976, 199). The actual practice more often begins with 60 percent as the minimum of government bills introduced, with at least 80 percent of them adopted (Peters 1991, 79–80). In Germany, for example, close to 85 percent of the government bills have been adopted, compared with less than 40 percent of member bills; of all bills adopted, government bills accounted for almost 80 percent (Table 5.1). The clearest consistent exception to this rule is the United States. Parliamentary systems tend to depart from this practice only when they have minority governments or unstable majority coalitions.

The cabinet has the right to propose legislation to parliament directly, and as a matter of practice, parliament and its committees spend most of their time on government bills. Some questions of public policy, however, do not come to parliaments at all, depending upon the constitution of each country. In Britain, for example, the government does not need parliamentary approval for foreign policy, capital expenditures, or even many aspects of economic policy (Ryle 1988, 232). In France, the Fifth Republic constitution limits the National Assembly's scope of policy jurisdiction (Ehrmann and Schain 1992, 329). In Germany, the Bundestag enacts broadly phrased legislation, within which administrative agencies develop more specific regulations and practices (von Beyme 1990, 359).

It is far more difficult for members than it is for the government to introduce bills. In Britain, members may not introduce bills except with formal permission of the House. As a result, there are elaborate procedures by which many members compete for the possibility of introducing their own bills, but once introduced, the cabinet controls the use of parliamentary time (Richards 1979). In Sweden, by contrast, there is a specified time during which member bills may be introduced without limitation.

Furthermore, it is far more difficult for members to prepare their own bills than it is for the government. The cabinet controls the agencies staffed by the civil service, who possess a specialized staff to draft bills. However incomplete their work may appear (see Box 5.4, page 90), they have a far larger and better prepared staff than do individual members for bill-drafting purposes. Not many parliaments provide a bill-drafting staff for their members.

In some parliaments, those nongovernment drafts with any serious possibility of consideration come from the major political parties, rather than from individual members acting alone. In Sweden, they are referred to the committees, which consider government bills and relevant party motions at the same time. The committees report their views on both the government bills and the party motions. The parties, in turn, work hard and long, and have their own party staff, in the preparation of their motions.

There is a greater scope for parliamentary activity in the preparation, and adoption, of amendments than in bills themselves. The German committees have been particularly active in considering amendments, with the result that few government drafts are adopted without change, more so than in either Britain or France. Yet, French committee activity in considering amendments, with government encouragement, has been increasing. Over 75 percent of the committee amendments are then adopted on the floor (Ehrmann and Schain 1992, 332–33; Frears 1990, 42–43; Schwarz and Shaw 1976, 210–12). By contrast, of 3,510 amendments proposed by individual members in bill

committees in Britain, only 171 were adopted, while of 907 amendments moved by ministers, all but one were adopted (Walkland 1979a,
288).

The U.S. Congress is the clearest exception to the generalization
that the cabinet monopolizes legislative time and product. The president and his administration do not have the right to introduce bills in
Congress. Draft bills are transmitted to "the Hill," but must be introduced by a member. Ordinarily a member will introduce an "Administration bill," but will sometimes specify that he does so "by request,"
signaling that he does not agree with the proposal. In Britain, the
nongovernment bill is termed a "private member bill." In the United
States, all bills, including those drafted by the administration, have the
status of private member bills in the British sense (appendix C).

The committees are the key working forum for the legislature to
consider government and other proposals. If the legislature adopts important amendments to a draft bill, those amendments usually are initially considered in committee. If the legislature rejects a government
bill, that rejection begins in committee. If serious interparty negotiations are to occur on government legislation, they usually take place in
the committee and at the time the committee is considering the bill.

Cabinet officials are actively involved in the committee stages of a
bill. In Britain, the minister leads the government majority in the bill
committee. The members may suggest amendments in committee, but
it is the minister who decides whether or not to accept them as part of
the government's draft. Elsewhere, ministers often meet with the committee as they consider the bill and possible amendments. The most
visible activity by cabinet ministers among democracies occurs in the
American congressional committee public hearings on proposed bills.

In Westminster systems, the minister usually leads floor debate for
the government, while the other party's leader controls time for his
side. In continental parliaments with permanent committees, the committee leaders often are in charge of floor consideration of legislation.

A very visible action by the chief executive in dual-branch systems
is either to sign or to veto a bill from the legislature. In parliamentary
systems, assent by the symbolic head of state is perfunctory. On any
controversial measure, the U.S. president will receive advice from all
sources, including congressmen, about what he should do. If he vetoes
a bill, Congress has the option of attempting to "override" the veto by
a two-thirds majority. Most vetoes are "sustained," as in the Bush

presidency, even though the Republican president faced a Democratic majority in Congress (Davidson and Oleszek 1994, 246–52).

Prelegislative Stages

Given government control of parliamentary time and product, some of the most important decisions about the content of legislation occur before the bill arrives at parliament. The "prelegislative stages" may be more important than the "legislative stages" within the parliament itself. The government may follow an elaborate procedure of first forming a study commission; second, referring the commission's report to public comment; and third, developing its own legislative draft, which is then formally introduced to parliament.

Usually, however, there is much less public knowledge about these prelegislative stages, and there is also much less published research, than there is about events and thinking within the parliament. Parliament is the publicly accessible unit of government.

Both Britain and Sweden make extensive use of these policy-formulation preparatory stages. The British have long used the "white paper" to formally announce and justify the government's policy intentions and legislative proposals, and more recently have formally developed a prefatory step of the "green paper." All Swedish government proposals first go through the royal commission preparation stages. Most are fairly simple and quick, but major controversies can take years through a series of commissions, which then prepare elaborate background studies and publish extensive reports of their recommendations, and, if necessary, their internal disagreements. These published reports then become part of the official legislative record.

The more important the topic, and especially the more controversial, the longer the deliberations of the study commissions. In Sweden, the membership of the commissions is a vital question; the major interest groups and the political parties will all be represented on the important commissions. In addition, leading legislators will themselves be members of the study commissions (Arter 1990, 124–25).

This elaborate prelegislative set of steps is not nearly as well defined or uniform in the United States as it is in Western Europe. The Social Security Commission of the early 1980s, however, was an application of this pattern to a very controversial issue in U.S. public policy. The inclusion of congressional leaders on that commission was one of the important ingredients of the ultimate success of its proposals (LeLoup and Shull 1993, 226–29).

A more common American practice, however, is for the preliminary stages to occur within the congressional committees. The committees initiate their own hearings and studies and negotiate their own proposals. When a committee—the whole venture can take the better part of a decade—has achieved a sufficient degree of compromise and agreement, a bill will be formally introduced and promptly referred back to the same committee that had developed it. Not infrequently, a committee member will introduce a bill designated as a "working draft" or "vehicle" for committee deliberation, in the expectation that the originally introduced version must be modified and is itself a stimulus to serious and detailed negotiation.

Most legislation transmitted by the president has, however, been generated from within the administrative agencies. In addition, the presidential advisory staff prepares major presidential proposals for congressional consideration. The preparation of policy proposals at the upper levels of the executive branch follows no set pattern, for each administration works differently. In some instances, there is broad consultation outside the administration with interest groups, external experts, and relevant congressmen (Kingdon 1984; Wayne 1978). In other instances, there is deliberate secrecy, as illustrated by the development of President Carter's ill-fated energy plan. Likewise, the gestation and preparation of President Clinton's health finance proposals in 1993 were conducted in private, which practice was then moderated after public notice and criticism.

One common practice by governments in the development of legislative proposals is to seek the advance opinions of interest groups and nongovernmental participants and experts. The interest groups, too, seek to influence government at precisely this critical, and oftentimes private, stage. Departments frequently have advisory groups to learn the opinions of interested outside persons, firms, and organizations. In Germany, for example, interest groups would rather shape the content of legislation at prelegislative stages than later; if, however, their views are not included in the government draft, they then express their views through the Bundestag committees (Steffani 1989, 319–26). The practice of departments of seeking outside-group views is a long-standing one, noted as a common practice in Britain even in the last century (Walkland 1979a, 250).

One result of either the European or the American approach to the development of legislation—the external study commission or the internal congressional committee—is that the chief executive is removed from the development of public policy. The chief executive is often in the position of accepting whatever compromise other actors can agree to.

Though the British system of bill preparation sounds organized and systematic, a recent study commission has argued that too often government legislation is prepared in ill haste, thereby creating difficulties for all subsequent steps within Parliament (Hansard Society 1992). Excerpts from the report are included in Box 5.4.

This report, commissioned by a civic organization, also observed that little is known about how government bills are decided and prepared; the whole process within ministries and the cabinet is secret. The report also noted that ministers of both parties have not accepted the most important recommendations of internal parliamentary "Procedure Committees" on reform of the legislative process within Parliament (Hansard Society 1992, 81). Exactly the same result has greeted Canadian parliamentary reform proposals (Franks 1987, 132–42).

Additional Working Relationships

In addition to legislation, legislatures interact with executives on review of administration and the confirmation of appointments. Decisions on taxes and expenditures, although also in the form of legislative bills, are made through special procedures.

Taxes and Expenditures

Although "power of the purse" is often cited as the historical origin and also rationale for the British Parliament, that body now concedes control over expenditures to the cabinet. The days of parliamentary debate time officially allocated to the budget are controlled by the opposition party, which prefers to debate major policy topics and to criticize the government. At the conclusion of the topical debates, the expenditures are officially approved by Parliament in a perfunctory, noncontested motion (Drewry 1988, 132).

The German Parliament, especially with the unique provincial governmental composition of the upper chamber, the Bundesrat, can resist

---

Box 5.4

Government and Legislation

"Parliament does not 'make the law'. That is essentially done by the Government which . . . secures the approval of Parliament for its legislative decisions through its control over the majority party." [para. 310, p. 78]

We emphasize "the Government's prime responsibility to seek to get a bill right while the bill is being prepared and drafted, not leaving it to be done by substantial amendments of its own when the bill is before Parliament." [para. 40, p. 10]

"The failure of all Governments 'to get bills right'—or more nearly right, before they are presented to Parliament has been, in our view, the basic defect in the legislative process." [para. 182, p. 47].

Hansard Society 1992

---

the government's initial budget proposals. A compromise solution is usually negotiated through a combination of party leadership discussions and the official mediation committee between the two chambers. These discussions can involve not only expenditures but also the sources and levels of taxation, as illustrated by the events of early 1992. The tax question was resolved in the CDU government's favor through a split within SPD between the national party leadership and the minister-presidents from its party in several *Laender* (*Frankfurter Allgemeine Zeitung* February 19, 1992).

It is mainly in the U.S. Congress that considerable time and controversy surrounds consideration and adoption of the budget, both in expenditures and in taxation. The committees that consider expenditures, the Appropriations Committees (one per chamber), and that consider taxes (the House Ways and Means Committee and the Senate Finance Committee) are among the most powerful committees in Congress. Especially during the Reagan and Bush administrations, the Budget Resolution and appropriations bills have been delayed, and bills have been vetoed. The budget usually has not officially been approved by the financial deadline (October 1), and in some years, both president and Congress have resorted to high-publicity speeches and actions before a final compromise had been reached (Franklin 1992).

Review of Administration

Reviewing and investigating the conduct of lower-level administrative agencies is the type of legislative activity that dictatorships are likely to permit. Even if an authoritarian regime prevents effective legislative participation in policy making or in budgetary matters, it is possible for the parliament to begin to raise questions about the efficient and effective conduct of agreed-upon policy. That is, without raising questions about the propriety of a given policy or its ideological justification, it is possible to ask if the policy is being carried out in the best way (Blondel 1973, 93–102).

Such questioning is most effectively conducted by committees. Thus, until the new departmental committees, the most active committee in the Westminster system has usually been the "Public Accounts" committee, which joins an efficiency concern with its financial audit jurisdiction. This type of committee is often found in parliaments of the British Commonwealth (Jain 1991). The Polish Parliament during the 1970s also developed systematic ways for the committees to question government ministers and to obtain information that the government was not initially willing to release to the public (Olson and Simon 1986).

"Question time" is a Westminster method to permit members to raise questions with government ministers on the floor. In Britain, the ministers take turns through a several-week period to face the House, while the prime minister appears twice every week. Time is always limited, and oral questioning on the floor can become more combative than informative, especially with the prime minister. The party leaders carefully prepare for each day's exchange, for the mass media, including the U.S. CNN worldwide, will more likely provide publicity to the questioning than to any other portion of the day's proceedings (Franks 1987, 145–60; Irwin 1988, 77–82).

Because time is limited, printed questions and replies are increasingly common. While any printed question might be "called" by the Speaker for oral exchange on the floor, the printed form is increasingly used in Britain by the members to obtain information.

Not only do parliaments, and especially their committees, question ministers and also civil servants, but the committees can investigate public policy topics without having specific bills to consider. The new British departmentally related committees often consider such questions without directly and publicly prodding the government to change its policies.

The U.S. congressional committees are not so restrained in their public posture toward the administration. Rather, they may very well develop their own policy preferences, and use investigatory hearings as a way to develop their own legislation (Olson et al. 1991).

Confirmation of Personnel Appointments

In most parliamentary systems, the prime minister is free to appoint his or her own cabinet ministers, although that choice is subject to parliamentary acceptance in some countries.

It is in a dual-branch structure that the legislature would have more of an opportunity to examine executive appointments critically. In the U.S. Congress, presidential appointments are subject to "confirmation" by the Senate, which is ordinarily routine. The president's first set of cabinet appointments is usually accepted. The only recent exceptions have been the rejection by the Senate, in a highly publicized vote, of John Tower as secretary of defense (1989) during the Bush administration and the withdrawals of Zoe Baird as attorney general (1993) and Bobby Lee Inman as secretary of defense (1994) during the Clinton administration. Judicial appointments are also subject to Senate confirmation, some of which—Robert Bork defeated, and Clarence Thomas confirmed—have been highly controversial and publicized (Abraham 1986).

More commonly, American administrative appointees will visit personally with each of the Senate members of the relevant committee, and after confirmation, attempt to maintain a friendly and working relationship with that committee throughout their tenure in office.

A Troubled Relationship

In no democracy is the relationship between executive and legislature satisfactory to everyone all the time. In parliamentary systems, the British and Canadian MPs resent their lack of power, while in the dual-branch structure of the United States, there are complaints about stalemate between president and Congress. The French pragmatic solution of "cohabitation" was their response to worries about the possible impasse between president and National Assembly, when each was controlled by a different political party.

The relationship is never a settled one. There are occasional disputes in the United States over the presidential veto power, for example. Several years ago, a minor crisis erupted in Britain when a junior minister refused to appear, when summoned, before a parliamentary committee. In new political systems of Central Europe, presidents and prime ministers act uncertainly about their respective authority. If, in some countries, the prime minister is accused of acting in a "presidential" manner, in others, the prime minister is accused of not being able to control his own cabinet. The European continental democracies have developed intermediate constitutional and practical working relationships in between the parliamentary and separation of powers contrasts.

The relative positions of executive and legislature are always subject to change and criticism in democratic political systems, whatever the constitutional design and however detailed the written constitution. The legislative–executive relationship is one of the big questions of politics and has no clear answer that the main participants are willing to accept. The participants constantly test one another and the outer limits of their constitutions, as they attempt to achieve public policy objectives through the institutions of self-government.

6

The Electorate and the Public: Elections and Interest Groups

If two knights were to represent each shire in the British Parliament, how could they be selected? In the modern democratic state, political parties are the main means by which elections are organized and conducted, and by which the affairs of state are managed. This chapter therefore returns to the earlier discussion of political parties in chapter 3, looking at parties in the electorate and in election campaigns.

In chapter 2, we considered the social profile of legislators, the demands of their job, and the different ways in which they think and act as representatives. Here, we examine how they are elected to the legislature and perhaps also how they remain there over a series of elections.

In the democratic state, representatives are elected by mass publics, not selected by small elites. While postdemocratic dictatorships (especially communist) utilized the mechanics and public symbols of elections, they carefully dominated the entire electoral process through the single party. In democracies, by contrast, competitive elections between two or more parties are the key mechanism through which decision makers are designated who can become "representative" of the wider society.

This chapter considers electoral systems, district systems, election campaigns, the activity of interest groups, and current controversies in the organization and finance of democratic elections.

Electoral and District Systems

Election systems are complicated combinations of several interrelated parts. One part is the distinction between proportional and plurality vote counting methods. Another part is the geographic connection between representative and voters: some systems are single-member districts while others are multimember districts. These two elements are often found in combination with a third—the party system.

Vote Counting Methods

The goal of a proportional representation system is that the parliament should, in its party composition, closely reflect the proportion of votes each party obtained in nationwide elections. This goal can better be achieved in multimember districts than in single-member districts. If, for example, ten members are elected from a district, and if there are also several political parties, it is possible to distribute the ten members in accordance with the party division of the vote within that district.

The single-member district system originated in Britain and is usually found in two-party systems. The United States and Canada also use single-member districts, even though Canada has three parties in at least a portion of the country. In a two-party system, the party with the largest vote in a district is automatically the majority, and can easily win the single seat. If five parties were to contest for the one seat, that single seat could not be divided into fractions (Ziegler 1993, 171–81).

A multiparty system usually prefers proportional representation and multimember districts. A "party list" is the election ballot, with the voter selecting among the several lists. It is also possible for the voter to designate individual candidates within a party list. The candidates are declared elected in the order of their names on the ballot, starting at the top. Party leaders are at the top of the list and thus have personally safe seats; candidates at the bottom have very little chance of election (Steiner 1991, 65–87).

There is a third electoral system, mainly confined to France among Western democracies, but newly adopted by several of the postcommunist states of Central Europe. Under the French majority vote counting rule, candidates run in single-member districts, from which an absolute majority of votes are required to win. In a multiparty system, two "rounds" are required, two weeks apart, for one election. In the first round, several candidates run. The top vote-getters (usually reduced to two) from the first round then campaign against each other in the second round. This two-stage election sequence with the majority requirement resembles party nominations in the southern United

States with a first and runoff primary (Mamadough and Van Der Wusten 1989; Schlesinger and Schlesinger 1990).

There are many variations on these general principles. There are endless disputes over, for example, exactly how the votes should be counted in a proportional system and how the votes should be allocated among the parties. There are also many efforts to measure statistically the effects of different election systems upon seat distribution, proportionality, and the number and size of parties (Blais 1991; Gallagher 1992; Lijphart 1990; Taagepera and Shugart 1993).

Consequences and Difficulties of Electoral Systems

One of the larger questions concerns the party system: does an election system itself lead toward a kind of party system, or vice versa? The answer seems to be more interactive than mechanical. That is, election laws are written by legislators and party leaders who calculate their chances under different types of election laws. Party systems do change; the choice of election system reflects as much as it produces those changes (Shugart 1992).

One of the potential difficulties of a proportional electoral system is that the results are not exactly proportional to the national vote; another is that this system leads to instability in parliament, as illustrated by the Weimar Republic.

One way to compensate for the first problem is to allocate some seats on the basis of proportionality in the whole country, not just within single districts. Sweden has this practice, for example.

The response to the other problem, of instability through excessive party fragmentation, has been the "threshold," the minimum proportion of the vote above which parties are admitted to parliament, but below which parties are disqualified. In Germany, for example, the threshold is 5 percent, while in Sweden it is 4 percent. In the 1990 and 1991 elections in both countries, the "green" parties then in parliament were completely eliminated, for they fell below the minimum threshold. Electoral thresholds have been adopted by several of the postcommunist democracies of Central Europe; given their many new and small parties, the result has been that up to 30 percent of the total vote has been cast for parties that are too small to qualify to enter parliament. As a consequence, that large proportion of the electorate has no direct representation in parliament.

Table 6.1

British Parliamentary Election: Votes and Seats 1992

	Votes		Seats		Index
Party	N	%	N	%	Difference
Conservative	14,094,116	41.93	336	51.61	9.68
Labour	11,557,134	34.39	271	41.63	7.24
Liberal Democrat	5,998,446	17.85	20	3.07	−14.77
Others	1,960,703	5.83	24	3.69	− 2.15
Total	33,610,399	100.00	651	100.00	

Source: Survey Current Affairs (April 1993), 89.

Germany has introduced an innovation that is now copied in several postcommunist countries. Half of the Bundestag seats are allocated proportionally within large multimember districts (the *Laender*), while the other half are allocated to smaller single-member districts. The combination of the threshold with this dual election system has been associated with the consolidation of the party system, averting the feared repetition of the Weimar Republic experience.

Reform of the election system is often advocated but seldom accomplished. A major difficulty is that the parties and members currently in parliament are the very ones whose consent is required to enact changes.

The current controversy in Britain is an illustration. The several minor parties, especially the Liberal Democrats, suffer from the "wasted" vote. Though they gather a sizable share of votes in some districts, they are rarely a plurality in any one district. They may gather close to 20 percent of the vote nationally, but win only a handful of seats with the current single-member plurality system. In the 1992 election, for example, Liberal Democrats won 18 percent of the vote, but only 3 percent of the seats (Table 6.1). Thus, they argue for adoption of a proportional representation system. A postelection survey asking voters to recast their ballots under several different election systems found that almost any other election system would have increased the share of parliamentary seats for small parties (Dunleavy and Margetts 1992).

Table 6.2

Canadian Parliamentary Elections: Votes and Seats 1988, 1993

	Vote		Seats			
	1988	1993	1988		1993	
Party	(%)	(%)	N	(%)	N	(%)
Progressive Conservative	43.00	16.40	170	57.63	2	.68
Liberal	31.90	43.50	82	27.80	178	60.34
New Democrat	20.40	8.00	43	14.58	8	2.71
Reform		15.60			52	17.63
Bloc Quebecois		15.60			54	18.31
Other	4.70	.90			1	.34
Total	100.00	100.00	295	100.00	295	100.00

Sources: New York Times (November 23, 1988); *Le Devoir* (Montréal) (October 26, 1993).

In Britain and the United States, the vote counting system is actually a plurality system. The candidate with the most votes wins. In the British two- and something-else party system, the winner may get 40 percent of the vote in any given district, with the other 60 percent divided between two other parties. In Canada, for example, in the 1993 election, the Liberals won about 43 percent of the national vote, which yielded 60 percent of the seats (see Table 6.2). It is only in the United States, with a simple two-party system, that the plurality vote counting method produces a majority result in both votes and seats.

There is frequent speculation about which electoral system encourages the elected representatives and their voters to be in closer contact with each other. The best that can be said is that all elected representatives in democratic systems pay considerable attention to electoral and opinion trends within their respective districts. The similar electoral and district systems in Britain and the United States, however, do not produce similar party organizations or campaigns in the two countries.

In the selection of electoral systems, there is a trade-off between representation of many different, and perhaps small, shades of opinion on one hand, and effective and stable government on the other (*Economist* May 1, 1993, 19–21). The problem of cabinet stability was discussed in chapter 5. Although great ingenuity has been poured into the

> Box 6.1
>
> **Matthew Effect**
>
> "For whosoever hath, to him shall be given, and he shall have more abundance; but whosoever hath not, from him shall be taken away even that he hath."
>
> Matthew 13:12

development of elaborate electoral systems, they all tend to have one common effect: they distort the vote. That is, it is not possible to reflect all small parties and all points of view of a highly fragmented society, in a legislature with a fixed number of seats (even if it has 651 seats, as in Britain). The electorate's vote is distorted in the sense that the smaller parties do not win parliamentary seats, with their small shares thus being added to the seats won by the larger parties. The "Matthew effect" rewards the largest parties with an even larger share of legislative seats (Box 6.1).

For example, Democrats in the 1992 U.S. House election obtained 50.8 percent of the national vote but 59.3 percent of the seats (CQWR April 17, 1993, 965–68). In Britain, with a two-plus party system, both the Conservatives and Labour gain, while Liberal Democrats and other small parties lose (Table 6.1). In Sweden, to illustrate a multiparty system, in the 1991 election, the two largest parties gained seat shares (1–2 percent), while the smallest party in Parliament gained the least, and the Greens lost all (Table 6.3). That differential effect was felt even though Sweden has a national set of seats to allocate proportionally, mainly because of the 4 percent threshold requirement.

Electoral Campaigns and Political Parties

Election campaigns sometimes appear to be a combination of circus and character assassination. The candidates and parties attempt to gain favorable public notice through a combination of pageantry and emotive accusations against their opponents. Yet, it is the parties' and candidates' efforts to reach the electorate that give average citizens their best opportunity to become informed about politics and to participate in their self-government.

Table 6.3

Swedish Parliamentary Election: Votes and Seats 1991

		Seats		
Bloc and Party	Votes (%)	N	(%)	Index Difference
Nonsocialist				
Moderate	21.9	80	22.92	1.02
Liberal	9.1	33	9.46	.36
Center	8.5	31	8.88	.38
Christian Democrat	7.1	26	7.45	.35
New Democrat	6.7	25	7.16	.46
Subtotal	53.3	195	55.87	2.57
Socialist				
Social Democrat	37.6	138	39.54	1.94
Left	4.5	16	4.58	.08
Subtotal	42.1	154	44.13	2.03
Other				
Green	3.4	0	.00	−3.40
Others	1.2	0	.00	−1.20
Subtotal	4.6			−4.60
Total	100	349	100.00	

Source: Current Sweden 385 (October 1991).

Frequency

Parliamentary systems permit elections to be held anytime at the decision of the cabinet, within some specified time period. In Britain and Canada, for example, elections must be held within a five-year period, but can be held anytime within that limit. As a practical matter, parliamentary elections are held every three to five years. In the 1950–88 period, Denmark among sixteen European democracies had the highest number of elections, at sixteen, while Germany and Switzerland, at ten each, had the fewest (Peters 1991, 65). Most countries now have fixed terms, of, for example, three years in Sweden and four in Germany. The two-year term in the U.S. House of Representatives is the shortest of any democratic legislature in the world and thus twenty elections were held in the same 1950–88 period. Federations also have state elections, often on different schedules from the national, and thus Germany, Canada, and the United States have more elections, and have them more frequently, than do unitary states such as Britain, Sweden, and France.

With the exception of Brazil (Mainwaring 1991) and the United States, election campaigns are managed through political parties. Parliamentary candidates present themselves as party supporters. The party organizations prepare election materials, decide how to use television, and raise and disburse election funds. In some countries, the parties are reimbursed by the public treasury for at least a portion of their expenditures.

Although elections culminate on a day (or two) of voting (often on Sunday), they are long events, generally divided into two stages: the earlier nomination stage, and the later and usually shorter general election stage.

Nominations

An important part of the whole election process begins long before the official "general election" campaign. Candidates are nominated for the general election ballot by their political parties. In proportional representation systems, the party leaders decide who will be on the ballot and, most importantly, the order of their appearance on the ballot.

In the single-member district system of Britain, the party controls nominations no less than on the Continent. While the decision is mainly made by the local constituency party, the national headquarters can also participate. In the factional battles within the Labour Party over the past twenty years, at times the national office's view has been decisive about which candidates to actually nominate for the general election (Norton 1991, 101–3; Ranney 1965).

Not much is known about what happens in district party meetings that nominate legislative candidates (Ziegler 1993, 96–138). One study in Canada found that, in the 1988 nominations, there was not much competition for nomination, and the major consideration seemed to be more of local concerns than the parliamentary party (Erickson and Carty 1991).

The major exception is the United States, where candidates are nominated through "party primaries." The "primary election" comes first, that is, before the general election. The several candidates who seek the party nomination appear on a ballot, with all voters who are at least nominally affiliated with that party eligible to vote. The U.S. nomination pre-election has become a full-scale election, with the entire ballot printing and counting process handled by public officials. Any endorsement by party leaders of a candidate would likely result in rejection by the local voters of that person, so the usual practice is that party leaders avoid showing favoritism toward any candidate until after the primary (Epstein 1967, 201–32; Sorauf 1980, 202–24).

General Elections

General elections, too, are candidate-centered in the United States. American candidates are responsible for their own campaigns. They raise their own campaign funds, employ their own campaign advisers and media managers, and run their own television commercials. The national parties and presidential candidates wish to encourage a favorable vote for the congressional candidates of their party, but their efforts are viewed as marginal. One result has been split party control between Congress and president for most of the time since the 1950s.

In proportional representation systems with multimember districts, the individual candidates may not be well known to the voter, while the political party is emphasized. In Britain's single-member district system, however, the party is no less important in campaigning and in voter response than it is in the proportional representation systems of continental countries.

European as well as Canadian and Indian campaigns increasingly emphasize the person and personal standing of the party candidate for prime minister. Helmut Kohl, Indira Gandhi, and Brian Mulroney, all incumbent prime ministers, have campaigned as vigorously for the election of their party members to parliament as do American presidential candidates campaign for themselves. While American presidential candidates do sometimes campaign for the election of senators and representatives of their party, their effect seems to be marginal. In other democracies, however, the increased emphasis on public campaigning by the candidate for prime minister is taken as a mark of the "Americanization" of their politics, or as evidence of increased "presidentialism" within their parliamentary systems.

Voter Response

Voter response takes two forms: first, the decision actually to vote or not, and second, the decision of how to cast their votes among the parties.

Voter "turnout" is higher in all democracies in elections to the national parliament than to lower office. Turnout is also thought to be higher in Europe than in the United States. The very different ways in which European countries and the United States count eligible voters, however, make a direct comparison very difficult. Voter participation in elections in the 1980s has varied among European democracies, from a high of 90 percent in Austria to a low of 73 percent in Portugal (Peters 1991, 161), and even lower in Switzerland at 46 percent (Steiner 1991, 87). Voter turnout for the U.S. Congress varies with the schedule of presidential and midterm elections: about 55 percent in presidential years and about 45 percent in midterm years (Davidson and Oleszek 1994, 100–101).

While some democracies require all eligible voters actually to vote (Australia is an example), most leave the voting act itself to the individual voter. In some countries, as in Sweden, it is possible to vote by "absentee" methods for a full month before the official voting day.

Voter choices among parties tend to stabilize over time within any one country. Especially in proportional representation systems, the vote among political parties changes very little from one election to the next. Vote swings might be larger in newer democratic systems, of which Spain is an example (Table 6.4).

Within single-member district systems, a small change in the national vote can result in extensive turnover in party control of legislative seats. This small vote with a large party effect is more noticeable in Britain than in the United States, because of the greater emphasis upon party in the former than in the latter.

In Britain, the party of the candidate is of far greater importance in how citizens cast their vote for MP candidates. Attributes of the candidates such as ethnicity and gender make little difference. Incumbency, however, does help the incumbent to a small degree, including MP services to constituents. Nevertheless, MPs act in office as though their activities, and especially constituency services, make a difference in their electoral fates, and the Conservative Party does identify and target Labour MPs who appear vulnerable to a strong challenge (Bean and

Table 6.4

Spanish Parliamentary Elections: Votes and Seats 1989, 1993

Party Names	Votes (%)		Seats			
	1989	1993	1989 N	1989 %	1993 N	1993 %
Partido Popular (PP)	25.83	34.82	107	30.57	141	40.29
Centro Democratico y Social (CDS)	7.91		14	4.00	0	
Socialist (PSOE)	39.55	38.68	175	50.00	159	45.43
United Left (IU)	9.05	9.57	17	4.86	18	5.14
Catalan (CIU)	5.04	4.95	18	5.14	17	4.86
Basque Nationalist (PNV)	1.24	1.24	5	1.43	5	1.43
Canary Island (CC)	.32	.88	1	.29	4	1.14
Herri Batasuna (HB)	1.06	.88	4	1.14	2	.57
Republica Catalan (ERC)	.00	.80		.00	1	.29
Aragone Regional (Par)	.35	.61	1	.29	1	.29
Eusko Alkartasuna (EA)	.67	.55	2	.57	1	.29
Union Valenciana	.71	.48	2	.57	1	.29
Partido Andalucia (PA)	1.04		2	.57		
Euskadiko Ezkerra (EE)	.51		2	.57		
Others	6.72	6.54				
Total	100.00	100.00	350	100.00	350	100.00

Source: Espana 93 233 (June 1993).

Mughan 1989; Norris et al. 1992; Wood and Norton 1992). One of the greatest changes in both votes and parliamentary seats occurred in the 1993 Canadian election. The governing party, Progressive Conservatives, went from 58 percent of the seats in 1988 down to only two seats in 1993 (Table 6.2). In the same year, three parties each received about 16 percent of the vote, but two obtained over fifty seats each, because each was geographically concentrated, while the vote for the Progressive Conservatives was thinly spread over the entire continent.

In elections to the U.S. House of Representatives, and also to the U.S. Senate in which the whole state is a single-member district for the one Senate seat up for election at any one time, incumbents of both parties are greatly favored for reelection. Incumbent advantage is not based upon any one attribute of representatives and senators, but derives from a combination of constituency service (known as "case work"), increased visibility in the district, and the inability of the outparty (for the district or state) to find capable challengers (Franklin 1993; Jacobson 1991; King and Gelman 1991; Squire 1992).

But American candidates, too, are subject to party trends. The party of the winning presidential candidate, especially in the first election, usually gains seats in both the House and the Senate. Some of those presidential party gains are lost in the next midterm election. The difference between "some" and "all" in the midterm loss phenomenon motivates congressmen and senators to attempt to please their constituents to insulate themselves from party trends. In both the British and American instances, as discussed in chapter 2, it was the newly elected members who placed relatively greater emphasis upon constituency services than upon national policy as aspects of their job.

As a practical matter, however, most legislative seats are not seriously competitive in any one election. In all systems, incumbents tend to be reelected. In proportional systems, they are at the top of the party list. In single-member systems, they are personally known and popular. In the latter system, a seat is most competitive when there is no incumbent; then the two parties have a more even chance to gain the seat.

It is ironic that the highest turnover rates in parliamentary membership in the post–World War II period have been in communist countries. In those instances, the choice belonged to the ruling party, not to the electorate. One way to keep a parliament inert is to deny its members the opportunity to gain experience. In democracies there is a constant balance to be achieved between competitive elections and experienced members.

Districting and Campaign Finance

Two additional but essential elements of legislative elections are districts and campaign finance, each of which warrants special mention.

Districting

We have already discussed single-member and multimember districts, which are electoral units created by a geographic subdivision of the whole country. With the exception of Israel and the Netherlands, where the entire country is one electoral district, democracies face the task of drawing district boundaries.

The boundary drawing task is usually simpler in multimember district systems than in single-member systems, for the most common practice is to use preexisting provincial and administrative units. The number of legislative seats assigned to each district is proportional to population size.

In countries with single-member districts, however, the task is more intricate, for there are more districts to be drawn, and fewer preexisting boundaries or units to be utilized. There is also much more discretionary judgment to be exercised, for the boundaries are pliable and, depending upon the exact populations to be included (or excluded), the party result of the next elections could be affected. Britain and Canada create special boundary drawing bodies to readjust the districts periodically to reflect population changes (Sanction 1990).

Districting in the United States is a two-step process. First, House seats (Senate seats are of course constitutionally allocated by state) are "apportioned" to the states on the basis of the census every ten years. As the second and much more intricate step, each state must then draw its own districts for the U.S. House. Districting is a legislative and gubernatorial action in accordance with the procedures of each state.

Accusations that each party seeks advantage usually abound at redistricting time. Recent studies indicate that states with single-party control do show a partisan bias, but nationally, the partisan effects tend to cancel each other out (Campagna and Grofman 1990). What seems a more clear-cut bias in the redistricting process is that congressional incumbents are protected, so that favorable voting populations are included, and unfavorable voters excluded, from any one district. If adjacent congressmen are of different parties, they might swap portions of their districts to each other, as an example. The fine art of drawing district lines, if one is critical of the result, is termed "gerrymandering" (Davidson and Oleszak 1994, 53–61).

Campaign Finance

Campaign finance, like the mass media, is often the target of accusations of bias, manipulation, and partisanship. Although countries differ in their campaign finance practices, all countries share the common experience of recrimination. Neither politicians nor citizens are happy with their current campaign finance practices.

Most democracies provide public finance to parties to ensure that all parties have a fair opportunity to make their case heard by the electorate. Parties are provided campaign funds at election time, and sometimes also financial support for their organization and functioning year-round by public funds. The twin purposes of public support for political parties are both to ensure fair elections and to reduce the potential influence of private money (Dalton 1989, 279).

Campaign finance reform is a perennial cry in the United States. The twin onslaught in the 1992 presidential election of Bill Clinton and Ross Perot elevated congressional campaign finance to a serious public issue. Watergate, twenty years earlier, had the same effect on financing of presidential elections, leading to the current system of, first, public finance of presidential elections, second, public reporting of congressional campaign finance through the Federal Election Commission, and third, the formation of PACs.

A specifically American practice in campaign finance has been the creation of the political action committee, or PAC. Now subject to sustained criticism, the PAC device was a reform stemming from the Watergate abuses in campaign finance. PACs come in many sizes and from many sources, but the essential purpose is to make it possible for persons to contribute money to parties and candidates in a way that is both legal and publicly known through reporting and disclosure requirements (Sabato 1985).

Congressional candidates are not equally financed through the current practices of private contributions, nor are political parties. The consistent bias in campaign finance favors incumbents of both parties in the House and Senate. Incumbents complain about the constant necessity to raise campaign funds from PACs, but challengers complain about their difficulties in raising the needed funds. Since most incumbents have campaign funds, what makes the greatest difference in elections is the amount of funding available to the challengers. Ordinarily, the Republican Party is better funded than the Democratic Party, but the incumbency edge, currently favoring Democrats in Congress, tends to even out the partisan gains from current methods of congressional campaign finance (Abramowitz 1991; Kenney and McBurnett 1992; Sorauf 1988; Squire 1991).

Much less is publicly known about campaign finance in other democracies than in the United States. There appears to be less public concern, and, perhaps more importantly, campaigns in most other democracies are managed by political parties, while in the United States, campaigns are directed much more by the individual candidates. Parties in other democracies, not the candidates, raise and disburse funds. The countries, however, differ in the extent to which funds are handled centrally by the main party headquarters. In Canada, for example, the constituency parties raise funds for their parliamentary candidates. The many constituency-level parties vary in their fund-raising abilities, depending upon such matters as the prospects of party victory, and the presence of an incumbent, which sound very much like U.S. elections (Eagles 1992).

Interest Groups

It is only in the last 100 years that persons and economic enterprises have become organized into formal private associations, which, among other activities, seek to obtain governmental decisions and actions. When such private associations do interact with government, they are termed "interest groups."

When these groups first came to public and scholarly attention, they were widely regarded as "pressure groups," and some observers developed a "group theory of politics" in which most if not all government decisions were made at the behest of the external groups (Truman 1951). Current views of U.S. politics portray a far more complex pattern of interaction within which the attempt to exercise "influence" is mutual, not only from group to government, but from government to group, and from group to group (Heclo 1978).

While the total number of interest groups is not known—although their numbers appear to be always growing—a recent survey of U.S.

groups active on two sets of issues found some 3,000 groups on energy issues and nearly 900 on health issues (Laumann and Knoke 1987, 98). By 1980, over 2,000 national trade associations, representing business and industrial groups, had established national headquarters in Washington (Ornstein 1990, 301). In Germany, over 1,000 associations were officially registered in the early 1980s (Mueller-Rommel 1990, 314).

Interest groups come in many different varieties, and the variety keeps changing. Some organizations are "peak" associations, which are federations of many other groups. The major labor union and employer organizations are examples. Most interest groups, especially in the economic sector, are fairly specific, based upon a single industry, or a single portion of an industry, or upon a specialized labor skill (Dalton 1989, 206–44).

Many interest groups are not based on an economic activity, but are concerned with a population group (especially ethnic minorities and religions) or with current issues such as the environment or abortion policy. In communist East Europe, some of the earliest legalized private associations were formed on ecology and pollution issues.

The full-time group staff, "lobbyists" in American terminology, have become a permanent and important part of the government policy-making process. As paid agents of organizations with offices in Washington, DC, they become as permanent as administrative agencies and legislative committees. Their full-time career staff develop as long a tenure in their jobs as do civil servants in the agencies, and legislative staff in the committees.

Most interest groups devote most of their time to the ministries. Most matters are, at any one time, within the jurisdiction of an administrative agency routinely implementing a policy. Interest groups concentrate on this continuous agency activity (Norton 1991, 177).

Their attentions shift to the legislature, or to the chief executive, only when needed. Within legislatures, interest groups tend to concentrate on the relevant committees, of which Germany is an example (Dalton 1989, 234–37; Mueller-Rommel 1990, 326–35). They would prefer to have a steady and harmonious working relationship with both an administrative agency and a related legislative committee than to engage in visible controversy at higher levels of government (Ripley and Franklin 1991).

The most common form of group contact with government is through the daily and unpublicized activities of the permanent lobbying staff. Group and government personnel can see each other frequently and telephone one another as needed. The lobbyist, because he or she engages in daily and personal contact with government officials, has the opportunity to develop a reputation of trust and expertise. That lobbyist, however, can also produce the opposite personal assessment. A senator observed about the staff of one interest group: "They're devious. They'll go around you. . . . You cannot rely on the word of their lobbyists" (Senator Packwood, R-OR, quoted in Davidson and Oleszek 1990, 285).

Interest groups probably are less important in U.S. government than they are in many other democracies. Private associations are more completely organized in membership, are more hierarchical in structure, and are more closely involved in governmental decisions in other democracies. Interest groups are more commonly "consulted," for example, in Germany, Sweden, and even Britain, than in the United States in the preparatory stages of government legislation and administrative regulation.

The existence and activity of interest groups are more widely acknowledged in the United States, however, than in parliamentary democracies. The major difference would appear to be that the relatively greater importance of cabinet decisions on legislation directs European interest group attention to the executive, which shuns publicity (Norton 1991, 168–69). The relatively greater attention U.S. groups give Congress exposes them to more publicity than elsewhere. Furthermore, interest groups in the United States increasingly seek to stimulate and orchestrate public opinion on legislative issues, of which health care became a prominent example in 1993 (Box 6.2).

Interest groups, especially in Europe, shun publicity. Groups like to be known for many activities, but "lobbying" is not one of them (Box 6.3, page 111).

In some countries, interest group involvement with governmental affairs is termed "corporatist," meaning that the organizations both help shape government decisions and participate in the implementation of those decisions. This pattern is usually applied to economic issues, especially to labor–management wage settlements. Austria appears to be the one country most writers consider "corporatist." The Scandinavian countries run a close second (Heidenheimer et al. 1990; Peters 1991, 165–92; Steiner 1991, 255–65; Ziegler 1993, 249–82). The more decisions are made in a government–group negotiation, the less the scope for independent parliamentary decisions.

Box 6.2

The Public as Target: Lobbying and President Clinton's Health Care Proposals

Health Insurance Association of America versus the Health Care Reform Project:

"The major emphasis of their [Health Insurance Association] campaign is glossy advertising and grass-roots organizing. The organization has set up an '800' number and telephone bank to get out their message that the Clinton plan would mean higher insurance premiums. . . . It is also encouraging insurance salesmen to give their clients literature." The organization ran a TV ad "showing a young couple sitting over their kitchen table grumbling . . . [about] the President's plan. . . . 'The Government may force us to pick from a few health-care plans designed by Government bureaucrats,' the spot said."

The Health Care Reform Project in response "assembled . . . a 'truth squad' . . . to urge local insurance companies to . . . pull the commercial, which they did today." The Executive Vice President of the Health Insurance Association "denied that his group dropped the commercial under pressure. 'We felt the ad served its purpose,' he said. The Health Care Reform Project is planning an expensive advertising campaign of its own . . . friendlier to the Administration."

Beer:

"Anheuser-Busch is outfitting its trucks with placards urging Bud drinkers to dial 1-800-BEER-TAX. Thousands of consumers have responded and then received pamphlets describing how the Clinton health care overhaul could drain their pockets if it includes 'sin taxes.'"

Cliford Kraus, "Lobbyists of Every Stripe on Health Care Proposal: Special Interests are Turning to the Grass Roots," *New York Times*, Sept. 24, 1993

Election System Controversies

How we elect our representatives presents a continuing set of issues in democratic political systems. In the last century, voting rights for all persons irrespective of property or wealth was the major controversy. Only later did issues of gender—"voters" had been defined as males—

Box 6.3

A British Group on Lobbying

"The Engineering Industries Association . . . with affiliates of some 2000 small and medium-sized mechanical/electrical engineering companies, does not see its main role as lobbying. . . . We help our members. . . . When the government gets it wrong, as regrettably it all too frequently does, then my members tell the secretary of state and will continue to do so. . . . We live in a parliamentary democracy. This means all voices must be heard."

Letter from the Director-General of EIA to
Financial Times, July 24, 1993

and ethnicity and religious identity become controversial as qualifications for the right to vote (Bailey 1971, 52–56; Gerlich 1973, 105–8).

In recent decades, a variety of other issues have become controversial in the election system. Continued use of single-member districts with plurality voting is a controversy in Britain, while continued proportional representation with multimember districts is a controversy in Italy. Japan uses a modified election system (several members per district), with contending solutions including the use of either only single-member districts or combining single-member districts with multimember proportional representation systems. In Britain, the issue centers on the question of "fairness" for the minority parties, while in Italy and Japan, the issue centers more on financial corruption (see Table 6.5).

Redistricting is a continuing issue in the United States and a relatively new one in Japan. In the United States, the current issues of congressional district boundaries are expressed in terms of both partisan advantage and ethnic representation. In Japan, the issue is expressed most directly in terms of urban–rural imbalance. The urban–rural imbalance problem was the major representation controversy in U.S. politics in the 1960s, resolved, at least in principle, through a series of Supreme Court cases (*Baker* v. *Carr* 1962; Davidson and Oleszak 1994, 51–59).

Even direct popular election is an issue in Canada and Britain. More seriously proposed in Canada, the question concerns the lack of suitable regional power within the federal parliament, in that the appoint-

Table 6.5

Election System Controversies

Topic	Country	Claims and Issues
Proportional representation or majority	Britain Italy	Partisan fairness Corruption
Redistricting	United States Japan	Partisan, incumbent Urban–rural
Popular election	Canada United Kingdom	Senate: regions House of Lords: democracy
Campaign finance	Germany Britain Japan Italy United States	Partisan bias Corruption Corruption Corruption Incumbent and party bias

ive Senate lacks power within the system of cabinet and parliamentary government. The definition of Senate power and its composition and selection are closely involved in Canada's efforts to define its federal system. In Britain, the much less frequently advocated reform concerns the nonelected House of Lords (Norton 1991, 311–19; Watts 1993, 298–301).

The major controversy, however, about many democratic legislative elections concerns campaign finance. Everyone agrees that campaigns cost too much, and that "something" needs to be done. There is, alas, no agreement on the "something." In the United States, the evils of campaign finance are expressed in terms of a mixture of partisan and incumbent bias, and, to a lesser extent, of group interest bias. In Germany and Britain, and even more in Italy and Japan, the issue is phrased more as one of sheer financial corruption and bribery.

There are no simple solutions to these controversies, at least none to which most persons of expertise and goodwill can agree. How to elect, with dignity and fairness, our representatives is one of democracy's more difficult issues. Our representatives, elected under existing rules, are the ones who must decide changes to those rules (Longley 1988).

Over time, however, our electoral systems and practices have changed. For example, the nonelected U.S. Senate itself agreed to a constitutional amendment in 1919, providing for its own direct popular election. Parliaments consisting only of males have, throughout the democratic world, legislated women's suffrage.

Summary

This chapter has examined electoral systems, consisting of the two elements of vote counting methods and district systems. Single-member districts and plurality voting tend to go together with two-party systems, while multimember districts and proportional representation tend to be found in multiparty systems.

Elections in most democracies are organized through political parties, with the United States, France, and Brazil the major exceptions. Parties and their leaders tend to exercise control over both nominations and general election campaigns. One result in all election systems, and irrespective of the importance of political parties, however, is the reelection of incumbents.

In all democracies, the growth of interest groups has been dramatic, if not entirely recognized by the public at large. If a few large interest groups are seen to dominate public policy making, the political system is termed "corporatist."

One of the more difficult problems democracies have to face is how to organize their elections. Although that issue is not always a major and controversial one, it never disappears. It erupts at times, and then becomes one of the most important immediate issues for the political system to define and resolve. Perhaps democracies are always unhappy with the way they organize themselves. Desire for change, in the name of improvement and more democracy, is one of the constants in the life of democratic legislative systems. Democracy is a never-ending quest.

7

Parliaments at the Beginning

As new members in a new Parliament, what should we do?

(An Estonian member of Parliament, 1991)

There is no good answer to the question raised by a member of the newly elected Parliament of the newly democratic and independent Estonia. A new parliament has to do everything at once, and its many tasks interfere with its ability to do any one them well.

Parliaments have become, in the postcommunist countries, the "central site" for the development of new democracies (Agh 1992; Liebert and Cotta 1990). Their autonomy and their importance are perhaps far greater in the new fragile democracies of postcommunism than in established democracies. The usual sources of power external to Western parliaments do not yet exist—interest groups, well-organized executive, and political parties, which we have discussed in earlier chapters. It is, however, within the new parliaments that these alternative sources of power will develop. Cabinets will be formed within parliament, political parties will grow out of parliamentary decision making, and external interest groups will be attracted to parliament as a power center.

A newly invigorated and newly established parliament in a new democratic political system is faced with the multiple needs to create a new political system, to form and interact with a new government, to revise either the economy or the legal system or both, and to organize itself for effective action. The newly democratic legislatures of Latin America have not faced the same task as Central Europe has faced, of completely reorganizing the economy. Perhaps more of the legal sys-

---

Box 7.1

Authoritarian System Transformation: Readings

Korosenyi, Andras. 1991. "Revival of the Past or New Beginning? The Nature of Post-Communist Politics." In Gyorgy Szoboszlai (ed.), *Democracy and Political Transformation.* Budapest: Hungarian Political Science Association.

Rona-Tas, Akos. 1991. "The Selected and the Elected: The Making of the New Parliamentary Elite in Hungary." *East European Politics and Societies 5,* 3 (Fall): 357–93.

Simon, Janos. 1993. "Post-paternalist Political Culture in Hungary: Relationship between Citizens and Politics during and after the 'Melancholic Revolution' (1989–1991)." *Communist and Post-Communist Studies 26,* 2 (June): 226–38.

Wesolowski, Wlodzimierz. 1990. "Transition from Authoritarianism to Democracy." *Social Research 57* (Summer): 435–61.

---

tem could be retained without substantial change as well. Perhaps most of the civil code and even more of the criminal code could be adapted with little change. In the Central European new democracies, however, all of these tasks must be done, must be done well, and must be done at once (Offe 1991). For a selected list of reflections by Central European scholars on their recent authoritarian system transformation, see Box 7.1.

New Institution, New Members, New Tasks

Every day, complained James Madison in the First U.S. Congress over two hundred years ago, we suffer "from the want of precedents" (Galloway 1965, 9). Doing things for the first time meant that there was no accumulation of experience in either how to create a new country or how to invent a new democratic political system.

In retrospect, the members of the First U.S. Congress had an extensive body of both institutional development and personal experience on which to act. There was little uncertainty in that Congress about how to proceed. There was even little uncertainty in the earlier Constitutional

Convention. Many of the members of both the Convention and the Congress had previously served in their state legislatures. The American states, though colonies, were largely self-governing, and the legislatures were active bodies, often confronting hostile appointed governors. The legislatures of the increasingly independent colonies probably were more active and autonomous bodies than was the British Parliament of that time. The newly elected congressmen had the benefit of personal experience in their state legislatures. Furthermore, the colonial legislatures were sufficiently similar to each other, based on the practices of the British House of Commons, that they had a common body of rules, procedures, and practices they could utilize in the new Congress.

Legislatures of Southern and Eastern Europe that have become democratic after a period of dictatorship or military government, however, are in very different circumstances. Few, if any, of the members have previously served in democratic institutions. Few, if any, have held freely elected office. Although most communist countries and many military dictatorships retained the form of a legislature, few of that legislature's practices and internal structures are adaptable to the new political context of democracy.

Yet, a legislature begins with its inheritance. There is usually a building for floor sessions, a variety of eating facilities, several rooms suitable for committees, a secretarial staff, a maintenance staff, and perhaps a library. Communist-era legislatures had the formal structure of several political parties of the Communists and several satellite parties, and of several committees. They also had a set of rules and procedures by which bills were formally introduced, considered, and voted. None of these characteristics were active or important during Communist rule; yet, they were the only existing resources for the newly democratized legislatures when their new members arrived.

The Members

Who are the members of the new legislatures of the postcommunist democracies? Those who were elected in the first wave of reform in 1989 in Central Europe may be very different from their successors in years to come. They were certainly very different from the communists whom they replaced.

The first wave of democratic legislators may be very distinctive in

Box 7.2

The Collapse of Communist Rule in Central Europe: Readings

Garton-Ash, Timothy. 1990. *The Magic Lantern.* New York: Random House.

Gwertzman, Bernard, and Michael T. Kaufman, eds. 1990. *The Collapse of Communism.* New York: New York Times Books/Random House.

Ost, David. 1990. *Solidarity and the Politics of Anti-Politics.* Philadelphia: Temple University Press.

Sanford, George. 1992. "The Polish Road to Democratisation: From Political Impasse to the 'Controlled Abdication' of Communist Power." In George Sanford (ed.), *Democratization in Poland, 1988–90.* New York: St. Martin's Press.

both their tasks and their attitudes toward and experiences in politics. One set of members in the first wave will have had leadership roles in the opposition groups. Or they may have been active and enthusiastic participants in the immediate anticommunist street demonstrations in their countries. The proportion of such members, who could be expected to have a positive attitude toward political involvement, might vary with the degree to which a country had been able to develop an opposition organizational structure in the first place. For accounts of the street demonstrations and the snap elections that led to the collapse of communist rule in Central Europe, see Box 7.2.

Another set of legislators in the first wave, however, may be accidental members, who were needed to fill candidate positions—which had to be filled quickly, and they were available through some type of participation in the reform movement. Given the sudden rush to reform in 1989, many of these persons found themselves elected unexpectedly to an institution that had little appeal to them, at least originally. In the new parliaments, they felt overwhelmed by their responsibilities and little prepared to fulfill their tasks.

A third set of members may be survivors of the old system. They became politically active during Communist rule, and have found a place for themselves in transformed circumstances. They may in the new regime be members of the postcommunist parties, and may, through a combination of experience and flexibility, become among the new parliament's most active and innovative members. Most persons now active in the new democratic politics were members of the Communist Party when membership was a requirement for either education or professional employment. Only some, however, have remained with the successor parties to the old ruling parties.

In occupation and education, the new members of newly democratized legislatures differed from their Communist predecessors. The largest single category of Communist system legislators filled quotas for women, youth, and workers. These members were replaced at every election. The longer-term members, who were the decision makers, were employed either as managers in state factories or were Communist Party paid staff, often in the offices of the central committee. The newly elected democratic members were mainly writers, dramatists, and others who worked with symbols, and whose occupations were not directly supervised by the state and the state party (Hibbing and Volgyes 1992; Loewenberg 1993; Reschova 1992; Syllova 1992).

This variety of new members in new institutions face the task not only of discovering themselves politically, but of building a new institution. They must do so while attempting to resolve the multiple policy problems of their new democracies.

Rules and Procedures

In Communist parliaments, the presidium was the formal body to make scheduling decisions and committee assignments. It officially included leaders of the several other permitted satellite parties in addition to the ruling Communist Party.

Newly democratic parliaments of Central Europe tend to continue to use a presidium as the official source of leadership. With the growth and fragmentation of parties, the presidium might become unwieldy in both size and procedures. As in former Czechoslovakia, a completely unofficial body of party leaders, the "political gremium," became a more efficient and practical means of coordinating agendas and schedules among the party leaders. This device was a return to a prewar practice.

In the Estonian Parliament, the vote counting rule was that a bill or motion required the positive votes of at least 50 percent of the full membership. This rule, during the Communist period, had no practical significance except as symbol. But in the completely altered political circumstances of new members and free debate, that rule became a powerful weapon in the hands of the minority. Since a large minority of the population in Estonia are ethnic Russians, this rule permitted the Russian deputies to paralyze the Parliament.

These examples illustrate a broader point: a revitalized legislature begins with its inheritance from the past. The rules of the Communist period continue into the new democratic era, unless they are altered. But to reconsider the rules and to find agreement upon new rules is a time-consuming and often frustrating task. The response of the revitalized democratic parliament, in its initial years, is usually to adapt and to alter the existing rules in specific ways and for specific purposes, postponing the larger task of reconsidering the whole system of rules and practices of the legislature (Olson et al. 1993).

One of Thomas Jefferson's lasting contributions to the U.S. Congress was his codification of the rules of procedure of the British House of Commons of his time. He wished to provide a firm and clear set of rules by which Congress could conduct its affairs and consider the public's business. The existing rules of the Senate and the House are, to this day, revisions of his initial set of rules (Oleszek 1978, 5–6).

Today's institutionalized committee system of Congress did not exist at the beginning; rather, Congress began with British practice and organization. The committee system has evolved through trial and error and with many revisions, but the beginnings of the current committee system may be traced back to the early and formative years of the new Congress in a new country (Smith and Deering 1984, 7–34).

The importance not only of rules but of standards of personal conduct is visible especially on the floor. How the presiding officer addresses the assembly and the individual participants can easily vary by the personality and aptitude of that person. The way in which that officer states the pending question, and the sequence in which he asks for the vote are, in established parliaments, a matter of settled order. In new legislatures with new members, neither the members nor the presiding officer may have a clear notion of proper parliamentary procedure. If several persons take turns as the presiding officer, variations among those officers may be considerable in a new parliament simply because everyone is new, doing everything the first time. As one person noted about his new parliament, "The voting procedure last week was a real disaster" (a Polish member of Parliament, 1992).

Standards of personal conduct are also visible and important as members speak in debate. In early 1992, one Polish deputy on the floor called the reformed Communist Party "traitors." The members of that party walked out, and the party leader threatened a lawsuit. One practice in tense international negotiations is that diplomats use the formal language of courtesy and respect; legislative debate is also often characterized by formal courtesies. Many legislatures have rules requiring the members not to demean one another or their motives. Depersonalization of conflict is one way to make disagreements discussible and resolvable. The ability of members to act civilly toward each other, and even to be friends, is sometimes very puzzling to the casual observer in either established or new democracies.

One strong incentive for the development of legislative rules that are considered fair and equitable by all sides is the expectation that the current majority party or coalition will be replaced by the current minority. The current majority in competitive systems must anticipate in the future having to live by the same rules it currently imposes upon the current minority. The same expectation imposes a discipline upon the minority's tactics of opposition and disagreement. A newly democratized parliament has never had this experience; it only knows how the Communists had dominated political life through the manipulation of ostensibly democratic rules and procedures.

Internal Organization I: Political Parties

One of the most vexatious problems facing a newly created democracy is the formation of political parties. In the sudden regime transformations in Central Europe in 1989, the leading organization was a broad amorphous "front," with no clear goal except opposition to Communist rule, and with no clear organization or membership. Crowds in the street, and gifted orators with microphones, were the means by which Communist rule was abolished (Brokl 1992; Garton-Ash 1990; Olson and Fried 1992; Skala and Kunkel 1992).

Within Central Europe, one of the few exceptions to the street crowd pattern was "Solidarność" in Poland. Molded through years of worker strikes and intellectuals' organization, and honed during martial law, Solidarity had been able to form more of a regularized organization with leaders, followers, and advisors, than occurred in any of the other countries. But it, too, was a very broad protest movement, held together by the force and symbol of its leader and by its common objective of opposition to Communist rule (Jasiewicz 1993; Ost 1990).

After the regime transformation had occurred in just one year (1989) in the whole region, a second but much longer transformation was beginning—the crystallization of political parties. Some number of political parties could be expected to emerge from within the broad social movements such as Solidarity in Poland and the Civic Forum in Czechoslovakia. These movements were too broad in purpose and too diverse in composition to remain as a single and effective governing force. The many practical decisions facing any governmental system would, in a democratic society, lead to differences of opinion within the regime transformative movements.

The Polish presidential election of 1990 and parliamentary election of 1991 illustrate the rapid fragmentation of the party system. Many small parties attempted to form and to find a popular following. About twenty parties won seats in the 1991 election to Parliament. The two largest parties—a group evolved from Solidarity and the reformed Communists—each won about 13 percent of the seats. Three different governing cabinets were formed within the 1991–93 Sejm. Although each was formed mainly from the parties that originated in Solidarity, their disputes finally led to the early dissolution of Parliament and elections in 1993.

Within both the Czechoslovakian Federal Assembly and the Polish Sejm, the original broad reform movements began to divide into smaller party clubs. Some of the party clubs continued to meet in a broader caucus of the regime reform movement. Some of the new groups within the parliament felt very uncomfortable with the concept of "party." They resisted the internal changes that term implied—a clear internal structure, a formal membership, and some clear program. There was a proliferation not only of political parties but also of different types of political organization (Olson and Fried 1992).

There may be several stages of party development in Central Europe. Once a democratic system has been installed, the first stage is the breakup of the initiating broad reform movement—the regime transformation movement—into many smaller groupings. We are also seeing the emergence of new parties that had little or no part in the regime transformation process itself. The first wave of party transformation could have been the division of the initiating broad movement into two or three groups. Instead, we are seeing the development of many small parties and other political groups (Berglund and Dellenbrandt 1992; Pacek 1992).

The second stage may take longer than the first: the consolidation of the many new small parties into fewer but larger parties. Divisions and splits come quickly; the development of unity and organization takes much longer. The consolidation process may resemble the "several-party" system of Germany or Sweden; on the other hand, the party system could stabilize into a multiparty pattern more like those in Italy or Denmark.

The Polish parliamentary elections of 1993 may be a step in the consolidation of the party system. Two parties by themselves obtained over a majority of seats, while the total number of parties in the Sejm, or lower house, was only seven (*Financial Times* September 25, 1993). Similarly, the elections of 1992 in the former federation of Czechoslovakia placed a small number of parties in each of the two new republics (Olson 1993b). Yet, none of the resulting governing coalitions are stable, and few of the parties, whether in government or opposition, seem stable (Fisher 1993; Vachudova 1993; Vinton 1993).

The potential leaders of broader parties may experiment with different types of political party structures and designs. The diverse social structure of Western Europe that produced competitive parties does not now exist in postcommunist countries. Communism produced a relatively flat social structure and prohibited independent citizen organizations. Neither the social nor the organizational preconditions of Western mass-membership parties exist. It may be that aspiring party leaders will develop new ways of reaching their potential voters, perhaps through the mass media. It may be that the instant availability of mass communications will result in party formations and election practices more resembling U.S. than Western European models.

Political parties emerge from an interaction between potential leaders and potential voters. In a new democracy, the effective political leaders are in parliament. The development of party clubs and other groups within the legislature and their pattern of coalition and alignments have become the initial set of candidates and parties to present themselves to the electorate.

In multiethnic states, and/or religiously diverse states, the task of forming broad parties and of appealing to a majority of the voters is greatly complicated. Not only is party unity threatened, but so might also be the unity of the existing state. Election campaigns can disrupt, as well as build, the unity of the state (Comisso 1992; Linz and Stepan 1992; Olson 1993b).

As of the beginning of 1993, the number of parties in the parliaments of Central Europe ranged from five in Albania to eighteen in Poland. The number of parties large enough to make a difference, however, varied from two and three in Albania and Bulgaria to eleven in Poland (McGregor 1993). Once in parliament, the members combine and recombine in new party formations. Neither the number nor the size of party groups remains constant in new democracies. The evolving party system, however, does emerge from the actions and calculations of political actors in parliament in the beginning stages, as has been noted in the transition, a decade earlier, in Spain (Gunther 1989).

Internal Organization II: Committees

In the previously quiescent and decorative parliaments of communist states, the internal organization of the legislature was little developed. The only exception was the Sejm of Poland, in which committee growth began in the 1960s, and had become a full-fledged committee system by the end of the 1970s. All of the members belonged to committees. The committees met fairly frequently, and had developed practices of intercommittee coordination and ways to extract information from a reluctant executive (Olson and Simon 1986). When Solidarity erupted in 1980, and the Sejm was confronted with rival draft proposals both from the executive and from Solidarity, it was the parliamentary committees that negotiated, and in some cases imposed, a legislative settlement (Mason 1991; Zakrzewski 1982).

The growth and institutional development of committees took twenty years in the Communist Polish Sejm. The democratized Sejm has continued the pattern of committees and its procedures. All the other newly democratized parliaments of Central Europe and also of the newly free republics of the former Soviet Union, by contrast, were required to build a new committee system upon a more rudimentary structure.

One practice from the Communist period that has been retained in at least some of the democratized legislatures is the Committee on Law and Legislation, or, in some countries, the Committee on Constitution and Law. This committee had become the central coordinating committee, at least in Poland and Czechoslovakia, for a wide variety of legislation that also lay in the jurisdiction of subject matter committees. This practice continues in some of the new parliaments, illustrating once again the retention of inherited institutions and practices of the past.

Staff Support

Inactive legislatures do not need professional staff, and perhaps not even many secretaries. The personnel employed in Communist legislatures—janitors, food staff, lawyers—may be close to 1,000 persons, most of whom need to retain their jobs in the midst of both political and economic change. The more important the job, however, the greater the question about the appropriateness of their previous service and political loyalties in revitalized legislatures.

One of the tasks facing a newly democratized legislature is not only the recruitment of professional staff, but the design of a whole new set of support organizations to serve the parliament. The chancellory becomes a much larger and more active body, with several new units concerned not only with bill drafting and an expanded library, but also with new sources of research and information for the members and the committees. The organization of these service units and their relationship to one another are both difficult problems to resolve.

Furthermore, new members are not always convinced they need a new staff and service structure. In both Poland and Czechoslovakia, for example, the new research units have faced considerable skepticism from members about their creation in the first place.

Provision of staff to the committees is a related organization design problem. New legislatures tend to develop a centralized staff organization, whereby committee staff are part of a central staff structure, more on the Westminster model than the decentralized mode found in the United States.

These difficult problems of internal staff recruitment and organization are greatly complicated in bicameral legislatures. Should the staff be centrally organized through units serving the whole parliament, or should they be separately created for each chamber? Poland and Czechoslovakia, in part because their bicameral systems functioned very differently, have answered this question in different ways. Poland is creating two separate staff support structures, separately for each chamber, while in Czechoslovakia, until the breakup of the federation, a single staff organization was emerging.

Relationships with the Executive

In new political systems there are few certainties. How a newly elected president, occupying an entirely new office, will visualize his or her proper functions is constantly changing. How the parliament will understand their and the executive's proper functions is also constantly changing. Some presidents like to be their own prime ministers. Some presidents propose their own solutions to difficult problems, and then criticize parliament for having a different opinion.

One special source of controversy concerns appointment of the prime minister and the cabinet. Which institution has the responsibility for nominating executive officials: president or parliament? If the president makes the initial proposal, must parliament agree? This question created considerable controversy and uncertainty in Poland between President Walesa and the Sejm. New constitutional provisions have regularized their relationship, so that the president nominates, but the Sejm approves, the governing cabinet (Gebethner and Jasiewicz 1993).

In the first several years of the new democracies, most Central European governments have resembled minority governments of Western Europe. They have not had a firm base of parliamentary support. The rapid changes in parties within parliament have rendered the usual distinction between government and opposition irrelevant. In some instances, leaders of new parties themselves have been cabinet ministers, and have retained their positions in the Government of the Day. The clarity of the government–opposition distinction will develop along with the party system. Whether the ultimate solution will resemble a majority government pattern as in Britain or Germany, or a minority government pattern as in Denmark and Belgium, may very well vary among the new democracies.

The Constitution

What the new parliaments should do and how they should interact with the president have not been defined either clearly or legally, for the constitution remains to be written in the newly democratized countries of Central Europe (Elster 1991). Presidential elections have been held to fill an undefined office. In Poland, the status of the Senate is also unclear in the absence of a constitution.

By mid-1993, only Romania had adopted a new constitution. The other countries quickly abolished the most obnoxious features of the Communist constitutions, especially the provision that the Communist Party was "the leading force" of the nation. Poland has extensively amended its constitution, beginning with the 1989 roundtable agreements between the Communist Party and Solidarity, and with its "Little Constitution" of 1992, has agreed to at least the outlines of a democratic constitution (Gebethner and Jasiewicz 1993). Upon the dissolution of the Czech and Slovak Federation, both new republics quickly wrote their own new constitutions (Pehe 1993).

Presumably the parliament is the competent body to write a constitution, but this issue is resolved differently in each country, as each responds to the exigencies of its own internal politics. The initial Bulgarian elections in 1990, following the collapse of the Communist regime, were for a Grand National Assembly, that is, an enlarged parliament with the responsibility to write a new constitution. That expectation was common in Central Europe; the initial task of the new legislature was to write a democratic constitution.

The constitutional ambiguity of the regime and its institutions illustrate the improvised and constantly changing rules and procedures within which parliament and executive must work. The rules are in the process of definition as issues are faced and decisions made. The decisions are often made in the absence of clear constitutional rules. As rules and procedures are improvised, they become precedents for subsequent decisions. Each new democracy is inventing a constitution, bit by bit, every day.

The Public and Mass Media

The public usually has little understanding of or patience with delays in governmental decision making. All of the problems discussed above are time-consuming, and usually evoke considerable controversy. As we commented in the first chapter, controversy and disagreement, the open expression of which is encouraged by democracies, are themselves a source of public dissatisfaction. Usually public opinion is much more favorable toward the idea of an active parliament during periods of authoritarian rule, than toward the reality of an active parliament during periods of democracy.

For example, during martial law in Poland (1981–85), the parliament, along with the church and the army, had a strong sense of public trust, while the Communist Party ranked at the bottom. The public now does not think nearly as well about their democratic parliament, even though it is now much more active and vital than it was under the Communists. Likewise, in Hungary, parliament has declined in public trust. In 1989, it was second highest, while the army ranked third; in 1992, the army ranked highest, while parliament had declined to fifth out of six institutions in public trust (Simon 1993b).

The relationship of mass media to the legislature is always a difficult one. It has become fairly common for television and radio to broadcast important floor sessions, and to report during the evening news on events in parliament during that day. When open disputes broke out in the newly active Supreme Soviet in 1989–90, economic production declined as people watched in amazement the daily sessions on live television.

It is far more difficult for the media to provide background reports to help the public understand the sometimes acrimonious and sometimes arcane behaviors within legislatures. In countries with publicly funded mass media, one of the decisions to be made is how to regulate the media. The new political participants in a newly democratized system might desire to obtain favorable treatment in the media, which would make the practices of news coverage still another controversial and unresolved issue ("The Media" 1993).

The "print media," newspapers and journals, have a greater opportunity than the electronic media to provide analysis and commentary, but they are often affiliated with one political party or least express one point of view.

The Former USSR

The fifteen republics of the former Soviet Union are now independent countries. They have their own armies and are getting their own currencies, generals, and postage stamps. They already have their own parliaments—of a sort.

Their parliaments have a very different immediate inheritance than do those of Central Europe. They were all elected in the early 1989 and 1990 Soviet elections, in which, for the first time, it was possible for non-Communists to run, some of whom were elected (Hough 1989; White and Wightman 1989). The Soviet Union, in the few years of Mikhail Gorbachev prior to its breakup, had the beginning stages of a newly active Supreme Soviet (Goldman 1991; Remington 1991).

Perhaps the clearest break with the Communist past has occurred in the three Baltic states. Yet, in two of them, former Communist leaders, running as anti-Russian nationalists, have defeated the leaders of the anti-Soviet reform movements. Clearly, however, they have won office in competitive and free elections.

The circumstances in the Russian Republic are far more ambiguous. President Yeltsin was elected in a popular vote in 1992. He has claimed that only he embodies popular will, for the existing legislature was elected in 1990. The membership was elected under a Soviet—though much liberalized—election law. That legislature, however, like the legislatures in Central Europe, began splitting into shifting factional groups, which may become the nucleus of future political parties in future competitive elections (Belyaeva and Lipekhin 1993).

The conflict between the parliament of the Russian Republic and the president extended to writing a new constitution. Yeltsin created an entirely new and improvised Constitution Drafting Assembly to by-pass the existing parliament. The immediate result was two proposed constitutions, one from Parliament, the other from the Constitutional Assembly. That impasse led to two self-proclaimed "democratic" governments and physical violence between the two. President Yeltsin unilaterally decreed elections for a new legislature, under a new constitution, which he declared valid.

Some of the characteristics of the Russian Parliament in the 1990–93 period perhaps illustrate features of other former Soviet republics. For example, many of the members were part-time in their attendance at the parliament. There was, in addition, a high turnover of members. At least some of the members were either seeking, or were attracted to, paid full-time positions, including the administrative agencies and the executive. The Russian Republic itself is a federation, and thus the parliament had two chambers, but apparently they functioned as a single undifferentiated body. The party and group formations within Parliament, as we noted above, were in a constant state of flux. Finally, the rules and internal structure were remnants of the old system, ill suited to new political realities and policy demands (Remmington et al. 1993).

The new democratic legislature elected in late 1993 could embark upon the same journey of discovery that the parliaments of Central Europe are now experiencing. Each of the republics of the former Soviet Union will face the same journey, but perhaps in very different ways.

Summary

There is an interplay between parliament and public. How the legislature organizes itself, and how it conducts its affairs—how it finds acceptable and regularized ways of expressing and resolving conflict—will be noticed and evaluated by the public.

Furthermore, especially in newly democratic societies, parliament itself is the leading example of what democracy is in practice. If the members respect one another's views, and can articulate clearly their own views without rancor or hostility, citizens have an opportunity to learn a respect for the lawful ways by which to resolve conflicts over public policy and future law.

Not only what parliament does but also how it functions are important, both to itself and to its society. The structures of decision making, and the rules and procedures by which conflict is expressed and then resolved, provide important examples to the wider society. A parliament, having to make many substantive decisions at once, also is in the process of establishing its own procedures for raising and resolving public questions. Its solutions in turn help prepare the whole population for participation in the public and peaceful discussion of controversial issues.

The new parliaments also face uncertain, unsteady, and sometimes hostile executives. They, too, undergo a learning experience in the new, if unsettling, ways of democratic governance. A Lech Walesa of Poland, a Vaclav Havel of the Czech Republic, and a Boris Yeltsin of Russia, are very different types of executives.

The new parliaments of new democracies suffer from the paradox of too much work to do and too few resources with which to function. They lack the internal structure of committees, parties, and rules to fully meet societal expectations and policy demands placed upon them. This statement applies with equal force to the entire new structure of democratic governance, to executives and legislatures alike. In the authoritarian system transformations, the post-Communist legislatures are overloaded but undersupported.

There is no simple answer to the question opening this chapter, but it is a frequently expressed lament by many members in the new parliaments of newly formed democratic political systems. It is also a constant question by the population as a whole. Perhaps the dilemmas and travail of the newly democratized legislatures of postcommunist society help us understand the beginning stages of the legislatures of established democracies.

8

Legislatures in the Policy Process

The extent to which democratic legislatures are active participants in the policy-making process of their countries varies with three broad sets of factors. While these generalizations are based upon research on stable democracies, these factors may also be useful in understanding newly created legislatures of new democracies. This review summarizes the themes of the earlier chapters of this book.

The three sets of factors related to the degree and means of policy activity by legislatures are:

1. External influences upon the legislature, the wider political environment;
2. Internal capacity of the legislatures to act, the degree of institutionalization; and
3. Policy attributes, the content and type of public policy issues.

Each of these three broad sets of factors includes several specific indicators (Mezey 1991; Olson and Mezey 1991b). The three factors and the indicators are listed in Table 8.1.

Characteristics of the external political and governmental environment vary the most among countries and their different political systems. Characteristics of the policy problems themselves perhaps vary the least across different countries and political systems. The internal attributes of legislatures are intermediate in the degree of their variation among countries. On many of these indicators, the British Parliament and U.S. Congress are very different from one another. The continental European parliaments are more variable in their placement on each variable (refer to Table 1.1).

Table 8.1

Factors and Indicators in the Policy Participation of Parliaments

Factors and Indicators	Policy Participation	
	High	Low
External		
Constitutional structure	Presidential	Parliamentary
Administrative structure	Decentralized	Centralized
Party and electoral structure	"Several"-party system	Two- and multiparty systems
Interest groups	Numerous specialized	Few, comprehensive
Internal		
Party organization	Autonomous	Subordinate or weak
Committee system	Permanent departmental	Temporary functional
Members	Educated, prior political experience, high tenure	Low education, little experience, high turnover
Chamber	Control own agenda, resources	External control of meetings, few resources
Policy		
Content and dynamics	Domestic issues, new, high visibility	Security issues, settled, low visibility
Stages	Implementation	Proposal

Source: Based on Olson and Mezey (1991b), Table 1.2, p. 19.

These three sets of factors will be discussed in the order of their importance, beginning with the wider political and governmental environment within which legislatures exist and function.

External Environment

The very rapid regime changes in the USSR and Eastern Europe in 1989–90 amply illustrate the importance of the wider political system in defining the circumstances within which legislatures are created and selected, and within which they function. It is the surrounding set of chief executives, administrative agencies, political parties, and also the electoral system and interest groups, with which legislatures have their most frequent and important interactions, and which, in turn, have the greatest impact upon legislatures.

The Executive

The key question in the analysis of legislatures concerns their autonomy from the chief executive. The executive is the chief immediate
source of constraint upon legislatures. To what extent does a legislature assent to proposals from the executive? To what extent can a
legislature modify and even reject such proposals? To what extent does
a legislature initiate its own policy proposals? In most nations, as noted
earlier, the 90 percent rule seems to apply: 90 percent of legislation is
initiated by the executive, and 90 percent of what the executive wants,
the executive gets (Dalton 1989, 313; Olson 1980, 174).

Among democratic systems, the distinction between a parliamentary
system with a unitary parliament–cabinet institution, and a separation-
of-powers system with a dual-branch structure, is the critical, but only
the beginning, point of departure. The United States and Britain exemplify the two opposite models, with the United States Congress the
deviant case among the world's legislatures in its policy activism and
autonomy from the executive.

Although both Germany and Sweden are parliamentary in form of
government, their parliaments have acted with a greater degree of free-
dom than has the British Parliament. The Bundestag has amended and
even rejected government legislation (Braunthal 1972), as has the Swedish Parliament in the 1980s (Isberg 1982). Furthermore, even the
British government was increasingly defeated on amendments during
the 1970s (Norton 1981).

Constitutional structure, especially on paper, is not a sufficient base
of understanding of dual-branch systems either. Although most Latin
American countries have the formal constitutional provisions, the
working reality is very different. The military has often been the major
source of power within the political system and thus the major constraint on the power of the Congress (Baaklini and do Rego 1991).

The Administrative Structure

The organization of the ministries and the manner of their decision
making vary in extent of openness and decentralization (Campbell and
Garrand 1981), which in turn can have an impact on the activity of
legislatures in the policy process.

The more open the process and decentralized the locus of decision, the greater the opportunity for legislative activity. While it is hard to obtain sufficient evidence on this indicator, it would appear that the legislatures of France and Germany have less impact, at least on monetary policy, than do the legislatures of Britain and the United States, in part because of how their executive agencies function (LeLoup and Woolley 1991).

Swedish administration is both decentralized and accessible through its system of advisory committees and decision-making boards. This system tends to produce legislative proposals from the government that have been thoroughly developed by advisory commissions, leaving little scope for Parliament. Yet, the system is sufficiently open and decentralized that members of Parliament themselves become members of the advisory commissions that work on controversial topics. The advisory commissions probably limit the government just as much as they limit Parliament (Isberg 1982).

Party and Electoral Structure

In most democracies, members of the legislature are nominated and elected through their political parties. The clearest exception is the United States, which has more of a candidate-centered electoral process than a party-centered one. France and Brazil, too, have more of a candidate-centered election system than is typical.

In all systems, however, members of and candidates for legislative office are alert to the electoral consequences of their actions. The U.S. Congress is not very active on monetary policy, for example, because the issue is not salient in elections. In Britain, to take an opposite example, MPs are active in the distribution of regional development grants because they think there is a positive electoral gain for them through that activity (Wood 1991). Members of legislatures appear to be very alert to public preferences within their constituencies, although it is not entirely clear how much difference is made in the election results by these local sensitivities. The more important the political party (through either strong organization or a party list system), the less relevant local electoral opinion on specific issues.

Interest Groups

Private organizations of persons, communities, or businesses often attempt to influence the decisions of government, and when they do, they are termed "interest groups" (Truman 1951). Although they are reputed to be more active and influential in the United States than in other democracies, there is little evidence to support that general comparative proposition.

The clearest difference is that interest groups in the United States spend more time and effort on Congress than interest groups in other democracies spend with their parliaments. In other democracies, the groups are more closely associated with administrative agencies than in the United States. The recent growth of parliamentary representation agents in Britain is an indicator of Parliament's increased policy activism.

In all systems, interest groups would rather accomplish their objectives with administrative agencies; failing that objective, they turn to legislatures. Even under a semimilitary government in Brazil, the computer industry's dissatisfaction with administrative decisions led directly to increased policy activism by Congress (Baaklini and do Rego 1991). In the United States, when congressional committees hold hearings on monetary policy, those bankers who disagree with existing policy will use the hearings to express their disagreements (LeLoup and Woolley 1991).

Most political systems would rather resolve disagreements among interest groups through administrative agencies, and behind closed doors. It is mainly in the United States that interest groups directly express their disagreements with each other publicly, through the forum of congressional committee hearings. They can also be very visibly involved in public lobbying of representatives when a matter comes to the floor for a final decision.

The formation of topically specialized committees in Britain, which hold public hearings, has encouraged the public appearance of interest groups to express their views. In few other countries do parliamentary committees hold public hearings, or even permit interest group leaders to appear before them privately. Canada, however, has recently formed parliamentary committees, with the intention of encouraging interest groups to make public appearances in committee hearings.

It is relatively easy for any governmental entity to make a decision when there is only one outside interest group that is active. It is relatively easy when there are several interest groups, if they agree. It is much more difficult when there are several active interest groups that disagree with each other. The general principle seems to be that legislative policy activity increases as interest groups are organized, are numerous, and disagree with administrative agencies and the executive.

In some democracies, interest groups and their relationship with the state become "corporatist," when monopolistic organizations decide certain categories of public policies in conjunction with state organs. These organizations are also often active in the administration of those policies. In this situation, both the administrative agencies and the executive, on one hand, and the interest group, on the other, attempt to resolve their differences privately, and to exclude active parliamentary participation and even information (Steiner 1991).

Internal Characteristics

The extent to which a legislature is well organized and well equipped greatly affects its ability to participate in the policy process. If a parliament is closely controlled externally, it makes little difference how it is organized internally. But if it has some latitude for independent thought and action, its ability to take advantage of those opportunities depends upon the extent to which it is internally organized. Its organization and resources define its internal capability for external action.

The main internal components with which a legislature functions include its members and the resources available to the whole chamber, as well as its structure of parties and committees. We will consider the internal organization first.

Internal Organization

The main means by which legislatures are internally organized are political parties and committees. Parties in a legislature are usually few in number, large in size, and relatively "strong," while committees tend to be more numerous, smaller in size, and "weak." Parties concentrate more on the organization of power, while committees work more with the substance of issues.

In externally controlled legislatures, few committees are permitted, and their actions are limited. In the most inert of legislatures, even political parties are prohibited. The Polish Parliament of the early 1950s, for example, in which even the Communist Party was not permitted to be organized, was referred to as the "Silent Parliament" (Burda 1978, 163).

In democratic parliaments, the place and importance of committees and political parties tend to vary inversely with each other. In the British Parliament, the bill committees are subordinate to party leaders. The U.S. Congress illustrates the opposite extreme, in which committees are largely autonomous from parties. Yet, the continental parliaments have evolved a structure that combines political parties—which do select prime ministers and do support cabinets—with active and important committees. The committees have delayed, amended, and defeated government legislation. How these committees actually function in practice varies with the party system, and with the cabinet's majority–minority base.

Political Parties

The number and internal structure of legislative parties vary among democracies. At one extreme are the two-party systems, illustrated by Britain and the United States. At the other are legislatures with many small parties, none of which have a majority, and among which unstable coalitions temporarily form a government cabinet (e.g., Italy, Denmark). Germany, France, and Sweden have evolved into a stable "several-party" system. Although no one party usually has a majority, one or two have a sufficient plurality to form the stable base for either a government coalition, or the opposition.

Legislative parties likewise differ in the extent of their internal organization and degree of centralization. Neither U.S. congressional party is disciplined or highly organized. British parties, though disciplined, do not have extensive internal structuring either, in comparison with the continental parliaments. The German and Swedish parliamentary parties have an extensive network of internal party committees. For parties in government, this structure of committees is a means of communication with and protest against the decisions of their own party's government. For the opposition, the committee structure is a means of developing their own policy positions against the government. For both sets of legislative parties, their internal committee leaders are able to negotiate with each other to explore the possibility of compromise solutions (Isberg 1982; LeLoup and Woolley 1991, 51; Loewenberg 1967).

The combination of these two characteristics is an important element in legislative policy activism. If one party has a majority, as in

Britain and the United States, and if both parties have a weak internal structure, decision making will flow elsewhere in the system. In Britain, decisions are made by the cabinet sustained by the party majority, but decisions are limited to the cabinet, not decentralized through the parliamentary party. In the U.S. Congress, the congressional committees are more the locus of legislative decisions. In Germany and Sweden, decisions are more made within the parliamentary parties and their system of internal party working groups.

Opportunities for legislative decision making are increased either by several parties and a consequent lack of a single majority party, or by weakly organized parties with low discipline. On the other hand, too many parties, and too little organization, would fragment the legislature, depriving it of any internal ability to organize itself (Mezey 1991, 207).

Legislative party linkage to the executive is a related consideration. In dual-branch systems, the legislative parties tend to be more independent of the executive than in parliamentary systems. Within parliamentary systems, however, the legislative party of the government is better situated to bargain with the ministers if it has a strong and highly developed system of internal party committees (as in Sweden) than if it lacks that internal organizational resource (as in Britain).

Chamber Committees

Committees vary greatly among democratic parliaments, with two attributes defining their ability to function in the policy process. Committees that are permanent rather than temporary, and committees that parallel rather than cross-cut the administrative structure, have an increased ability both to know and to act in the policy process independently of the executive (Lees and Shaw 1979; Olson and Mezey 1991b, 14–15).

Committees of the U.S. Congress exemplify permanent committees, which parallel the structure of administrative agencies, while bill committees of the British House of Commons exemplify the latter. The British reforms of 1979 and similar reforms in Canada in 1985 made an important distinction among the purposes and types of committees. Both reforms created a system of permanent committees to parallel the structure of ministries. In Britain, this new set of committees was limited to the review of administration, while the previous set of ad hoc bill committees was retained to consider legislation.

Legislative committees are constitutionally specified in Sweden and France. In the French National Assembly, they are limited in number to six, and are large in membership and broad (that is, vague) in jurisdiction. In the Swedish Riksdag, the fifteen committees are small in membership and have a specified jurisdiction. The French provisions help ensure a weak Assembly against the executive, while the Swedish system permits, but does not guarantee, an active and well-informed committee system (Ehrmann and Schain 1992, 333; Olson et al. 1983).

One reason why committees can become active and independent in the policy process is that partisanship can be relaxed in committees more than is possible on the floor. The small size permits personal friendships to form across party lines, and the lack of publicity encourages personal candor. Furthermore, the experience of working together over time encourages a common view against outsiders such as administrative agencies, government ministers, or even the leaders of their own legislative parties.

Chamber committees can become the means by which parties negotiate with each other (Steffani 1990). Legislative parties with their own specialized internal committee system, discussed above, place the leaders of those internal committees on the chamber committees with similar jurisdiction. Thus, the experts and leaders from the several parties are able to interact with one another frequently, and to develop personal relationships across party lines. The personal offices of those particular members, and other places of personal meeting and discussion, become the places and the occasions for cross-party agreements to be explored.

Chamber committees can develop close working relationships with the administrative agencies within their jurisdiction. Those issues in American politics about which the one relevant agency and the one corresponding congressional committee are in substantial agreement with one another tend to be resolved at their level, not creating controversy that would force the issue up within the political structure to either the chief executive or the congressional party leaders (Ripley and Franklin 1991). The fear of this type of mutually supportive relationship was one reason given in Britain for opposing the creation of the ministry-specific review committees in the 1979 reforms.

A system of permanent committees, with a defined jurisdiction and with durable membership, provides legislators with the essential resources of time and experience to become familiar with the substantive issues within the jurisdiction of the committee. They also become familiar with the administrative agencies and the interest groups involved on their policy matters. If the party system permits the reelection of incumbents, a legislature with permanent committees may become a more experienced body on policy questions than is the cabinet, with its constant rounds of ministerial changes.

Members

The amazement of the new members of the newly democratized parliaments of Central Europe and their stunned realization of the complexity of their tasks highlight the critical importance of the human beings who become legislators and representatives.

Changes in the membership of the British House of Commons over several decades have been noted as the basis for the development of a specialized and active committee system. The prior training and occupational experience of the members conditions their reactions to their unusual work environment and their desire to introduce change.

The prior political and governmental experience of members is highly relevant to their ability to function in the national legislature. If they have been elected to other and lower office, they are already familiar with election campaigns, party leadership, aggrieved constituents, and organized interest groups. Characteristics of the individual members taken together also are an attribute of the whole institution. A solid core of experienced members can contribute to the capacity of the legislature to think and act independently of the chief executive. A high turnover of members, coupled with low degrees of internal organization, helps build a subservient parliament.

Chamber Resources

The ability of a parliament to meet for a good part of a year and to set its own agenda is an important, if elemental, resource in the development of autonomous legislatures. Although the government sets the bulk of the legislative agenda, some parliaments have latitude to select their own issues as well.

The amount of staff, research facilities, and even secretarial support are basic to an independent legislature and its members. Several parliaments have considerably expanded the range and extent of their facilities for members and committees (Damgaard 1992). Not all parliaments even provide individual offices for their members.

Policy Attributes

The broad distinction between foreign and domestic policy suggests that how the executive and the legislature work varies in part with the type of issue under consideration. It may also be that the substantive content of policy imposes a commonality across national boundaries and even across political systems; housing and highways as issues, for example, may share more similarities across countries than with each other within any single country.

Content and Dynamics

Although there are many categorizations of types of public issues, it would appear that legislatures are more active on issues affecting the distribution of benefits and on the propagation of values, but less active on issues of either security (foreign or internal) or macroeconomic policy. The French constitution limits jurisdiction to only some types of issues (Ehrmann and Schain 1992, 329–31).

Issues also differ in the ways in which they rise to governmental attention. Some issues are highly visible and important to a wide public, while others are less visible and less recognized. On some issues, a wide variety of contentious interest groups become active, while on others, groups are relatively inactive. Furthermore, old issues become regularized in the specific legislative committees and administrative agencies that handle them, while newer issues tend to be both more controversial and less settled in the structure and procedures of their resolution. Legislatures tend to be more active on the newer and more controversial issues, and on those that arouse disagreement among interest groups, and less active on older and less controversial issues.

Policy Stages

Policy proposals are frequently prepared within administrative agencies and/or by outside advisory commissions. While their proposals, especially if unanimous, may leave the parliament little choice in accepting the proposal, the very existence of an advisory commission is itself an opportunity for parliamentary awareness as well as participation.

Once adopted, a policy is then implemented by one or more administrative agencies. It is at this stage that legislative activity is often found even in authoritarian political systems. Individual legislators can actively attempt to gain benefits for people and businesses within their constituency. Committees can review how the ministry has been implementing a policy throughout the whole country. Examination of policy at this stage of the policy cycle by legislatures is less threatening to executives than is involvement at earlier stages, which is why the prime minister permitted the British Parliament to create permanent committees for agency review but not for consideration of legislation (Johnson 1988; Norton 1981).

It is the committee system of the U.S. Congress that permits Congress actively to initiate policy proposals, as well as to counter executive proposals effectively. Congress's active formulation of future legislation is an exception because its committee system is an exception to the usual patterns in democratic legislatures (Moe and Teel 1970; Orfield 1975).

Conclusions

A legislature can be a working body. It can play a vital part in the governance of a state. There is, however, no guarantee, even in a democracy, that a legislature will achieve that potential.

If the members of a legislature meet occasionally, sit passively while the leaders read speeches, and then quickly vote in unison, that legislature is inactive and ineffective. If the legislature meets longer, but its rules and procedures are unpredictable, and various leaders present programs calling for immediate acceptance, that legislature, too, is ineffective. In the 1980s and 1990s, many countries have become democratic—sometimes suddenly. In nondemocratic systems, the military, the party, or the religious leadership may seize power, and, if a legislature is not abolished, it is limited to a public display function.

Yet, once created, a legislature has the possibility to grow within an authoritarian system, to develop various ways by which it can become more active than originally intended: the Congress of Brazil under military dictatorship and the Polish Sejm under Communist Party rule are examples (Baaklini and do Rego 1991; Mason 1991; Olson and Simon 1986).

The internal structures of parties and committees provide the means by which a legislature can act. If there is only one party, or if there is a continuous single majority party, or if the several parties are externally controlled, the legislature has little opportunity to develop an autonomous existence. If, on the other hand, there are many small parties, with persistent fragmentation of its organization and policy preferences, the legislature lacks the means either to formulate or to act upon a clear course of action. One of the important developments in both Brazil and Poland was the evolution of committees with the capacity to question the executive and to form their own views of proper public policy.

The external factors of control and the internal factors of inner organization flow together in the evolution of a legislature. It is no accident that prime ministers within Westminster systems have consistently opposed the formation of permanent investigatory and legislative committees.

Successful and active legislatures, like democratic political systems, are not created overnight. Even the more stable and long-lived democracies change their practices of governing. While there is a clear historical continuity between the first and the current U.S. Congress, and while there is a clear continuity between the early and the current Swedish Riksdag, there have been, as well, many experiments and changes over the decades and centuries. The quest for better government, for more democratic government, and for more effective policies is a never-ending search. Legislatures are at the vortex of that persistent self-dissatisfaction and that unceasing search for reform, characteristic of democratic political systems.

The hypotheses and generalizations about democratic legislatures presented here are a summary of many studies. Research has accumulated over many decades on a variety of issues in a variety of countries. Unfortunately, the many studies are not consistent with each other in the questions they raise or in the methods they use, or in the data they assemble. Even for research on the U.S. Congress, we can lament the lack of "additive" research, and the need to enquire further.

The comparative study of legislatures is at a much earlier beginning point. Now that newly created and transformed democratic legislatures are emerging in Latin America, the former Warsaw Pact region, and Africa, we have new opportunities and challenges to closely monitor and understand the dynamic of legislative organization and action in constantly changing democratic political systems.

Appendix A

Stages of Legislative Procedure

Each parliament develops a series of steps through which legislation proceeds to regularize the work of the parliament and also to ensure full and fair consideration of proposed bills.

The usual pattern among democratic legislatures is that the major legislative steps alternate: floor, committee, floor (Table A.1). Bills are "introduced" formally to the parliament "on the floor." They are then referred to committees, and from committees, are "reported" back to the floor for authoritative debate and voting. In bicameral parliaments, this sequence is repeated separately in each chamber, and then additional steps are required to reconcile differences between the chambers. If the chief executive exercises independent judgment to sign legislation, still additional steps are required to permit the legislature to "override" the executive's veto.

It is ironic that the final and authoritative steps, debate and voting by the whole chamber, are the most ritualistic and predictable portion of the entire procedure. Ritualistic, in that the presiding officer repeats certain phrases at stipulated points in the proceedings, particularly at the end and beginning, and during times to vote. If the presiding officer does not pronounce the correct words at the proper times, the whole chamber is thrown into disarray.

These final floor stages are also the most predictable for two reasons. First, the main arguments, and the leaders who present the arguments, have already been active at the earlier committee stage. Second, party-disciplined voting usually ratifies the agreements made earlier by the party leaders on the specific bill under consideration.

The general principle for the exercise of influence seems to be that

Table A.1

Steps in Legislative Procedure in Selected Legislatures

Legislature	Floor	Committee		Floor	
U.S. House	Introduction, Refer to committee.	Filter, Hearings, Report	Rules Committee	Committee of Whole: debate, amendments. Readings 1, 2	Final passage. Reading 3
U.S. Senate	Introduction, Refer to committee. Readings 1, 2	Filter, Hearings, Report		Debate, amendments.	Final passage. Reading 3
British Commons	Introduction, Debate, Vote. Readings 1, 2	Amendments		Report stage; Debate, amendments.	Final passage. Reading 3
Germany	Introduction, Debate, Refer to committee. Reading 1	Filter, Report		Debate, amendments. Reading 2	Debate, amendments, final passage. Reading 3

the earlier discussions take place within the set of steps in legislative procedure, the greater the flexibility of other participants to consider and agree to various proposals.

We begin this discussion of legislative steps with the events that occur prior to a bill's formal introduction to the legislature, the "pre-legislative" stages, and conclude with an executive's veto.

1. Preparation

The preparation of a bill can take longer and can be more complicated than is action within the legislature.

Most serious bills are prepared within the executive. On complicated topics, the British use the device of a "white paper" and an earlier "green paper" to solicit public advice on the contents of future policy. The Swedish government, and sometimes the British, use a "royal commission" to prepare legislative proposals. In the U.S. Congress, these preliminary stages often occur within the congressional committees. Committees initiate their own studies and public hearings on public policy topics, sometimes with the declared intention of developing future legislation.

2. Introduction

Formal "introduction" of a bill is a cursory step in most parliaments. A brief speech, a formal announcement to the Speaker, and especially a written notice in the printed transcript of floor proceedings, are the usual means for giving formal notice to all members.

One exception to this cursory procedure is the British "private member" bill, which requires special procedures and formal permission of the House. The governing cabinet usually controls parliamentary time, and it, not the individual member, has the right to use the formal and cursory procedure of quick introduction.

The unlimited right of members of the U.S. Congress produces thousands of bills—up to 20,000—in a single two-year period. Swedish members, likewise, may introduce "motions" without formal permission, but are limited to a specific time period relatively early in a session.

3. Referral to Committee

Parliaments differ in the means and timing of the reference of a bill to
a committee. The thousands of bills in the U.S. Congress are immediately referred to the permanent committees. They are referred without
debate. The committees have full discretionary powers over all bills
within their jurisdiction. One of their important functions is to filter
out most bills on which no action will be taken. Instead, the committees select those few bills to which they will devote their time and
energies.

Westminster parliaments have a very different procedure, rationale,
and organization. Bills are held on the floor for a "second reading,"
after which they are referred to a committee. The second reading is the
debate and vote on the bill "in principle." If the House agrees to accept
a bill in principle, then the legislative committee has a limited task: to
work on details and consider amendments. For this limited purpose,
the temporary ad hoc bill committee is sufficient.

Committees are very different in the British Parliament from those
in the U.S. Congress because the scope of their discretionary powers is
very different. Congressional committees have full powers over bills,
while Westminster bill committees have temporary and limited jurisdiction.

The continental committees usually have wide powers of discretion
over legislation but they are also usually required to report all proposed
bills and amendments back to the chamber.

4. In Committee

Committees typically consider bills and amendments, and agree to a
single text commanding the support of a majority of its members. That
majority is usually the result of interparty agreements negotiated by the
party leaders on the relevant committee. All of the interparty negotiations and most of the committee meetings are held in private.

The British bill committee meets in public. The party sides are led
by the government minister and his or her opposition counterpart. Even
if the two party sides disagree on the principle of the bill, the committee is limited to questions of detail. Party discipline will protect the
government on the whole bill, and also on amendments if the minister
insists.

Congressional committees in the United States do nothing on most bills referred to them. For the few bills on which action does occur, the public hearing is the most visible step, resulting in a printed committee "report," and sometimes receiving extensive mass media coverage.

5. The Decision to Go to the Floor

Whether parliaments meet for two days per month or throughout the entire year, there is never enough time for the whole chamber "on the floor" to consider everything. At the very least, parliaments develop a procedure and a decision-making body to allocate floor time.

The more controversial the measure, the more elaborate the time allocation procedures. In two-party chambers, the majority party clearly controls access to and time on the floor. In multiparty chambers, a council of party leaders, under a variety of names, usually makes this type of procedural decision.

The busier the legislature, the more detailed the procedures both to obtain access to the floor and about the use of floor time itself. In the U.S. House of Representatives, the Rules Committee fulfills that dual task for most legislation. In the Senate, by contrast, the whole chamber develops ad hoc procedures and time limits on each bill through a combination of "unanimous consent agreements" and "cloture" votes.

6. On the Floor

Usually debate and voting are managed by the leaders designated by the legislative committee considering the bill at the committee stage. Continental parliaments may use "rapporteurs" from the committee, while in the U.S. Congress, the committee (or subcommittee) chairperson and the ranking minority member manage time for their respective party sides of the chamber. Characteristic of the Westminster emphasis upon majority government, floor debate and voting are controlled by the minister and the opposition counterpart. In all cases, however, the pattern of committee leadership is repeated at the floor stage.

Legislatures differ in their use of time during a day and even a week. The U.S. House of Representatives typically considers a bill in one afternoon, with the major votes occurring toward the end of the afternoon (e.g., 4–6 P.M.). The U.S. Senate can take two weeks on the same bill, and voting can occur at any time. In the British House of Commons, the major vote of the day usually occurs at 10 P.M., while in the Canadian House of Commons—also a Westminster type of parliament—the major votes occur in the late afternoon.

Voting procedures also differ among legislatures. Increasingly, they use various forms of electronic voting both to speed procedure and to provide an accurate count. But many votes are by less formal and even quicker methods, such as voice, standing, show of hands, and the like. The most detailed vote methods record the vote by member name, termed a "roll call" in Congress and a "division" in the Westminster parliaments.

7. Resolving Interchamber Differences

In bicameral systems, special procedures are required to obtain agreement of both chambers on a single text. Westminster parliaments (and the Polish) use the "shuttle" method; the amended text from the second chamber is revoted in the first. If the first insists upon its original text, the second chamber revotes. The bill goes ("shuttles") back and forth between the chambers.

The U.S. and the German legislatures employ a special committee device to develop a single text, which is then voted by each chamber.

8. The Veto and Beyond

If the chief executive, unlike most of today's royalty, exercises independent discretion over legislation, that official has the option of either accepting or rejecting a bill from the legislature. If a bill is vetoed, additional procedures and steps are required to permit the legislature to decide its course of action.

Not all vetoed bills, at least in the U.S. Congress, are reconsidered. If the congressional leaders concerned with a bill think it advisable, the veto will be brought to the chamber to attempt a two-thirds "override" vote. This extra large majority is required in both chambers to enact a law over a presidential veto. Most vetoes are "sustained," that is, the president's veto is not overridden and the bill is finally defeated. Few bills, however, are vetoed.

This sequence of eight steps is a brief outline of a very complicated sequence of stages and procedures. The legislative history of every bill is unique in detail, for legislators, and sometimes chief executives, constantly improvise to gain their objectives. This outline is like a skeleton: the flesh and blood of people and of real activity must be added, but the skeleton provides the basis for life.

Appendix B

The Vocabulary of Parliaments and Legislatures

Backbenchers   Members of parliament who are not party leaders; originates in seating arrangements of British Parliament; *see* frontbenchers.

Bicameral/ism   A legislature with two chambers or houses; contrasted with unicameralism. The United States, Canada, and France are examples.

Bill committee   Legislative committee that considers legislation; contrasted with departmental committees; used in Westminster systems.

Caucus   General term for legislative party meetings; specific name for U.S. House Democratic party organization.

Cohabitation   Relatively amicable relations between a president of one party and a parliament with a different party majority; French.

Conference committee   Used in some bicameral parliaments to reconcile differences between the two chambers on a bill.

Confidence   *See* no confidence, vote of.

Cross the floor   Change of party by legislator; British term.

Departmental committees   British parliamentary committees to review actions of ministries or departments of administration.

Dual-branch structure   U.S. system of two independent institutions of Congress and executive branch; separation of powers.

Floor   (1) The room in which all members of a legislature meet; (2) a stage in legislative consideration.

Fraktion   Legislative party; German term.

Frontbenchers   Legislators who are party leaders; originates in seating arrangements of British Parliament; *see* backbenchers.

Government   Chief executive and cabinet; British and European usage. Also: Government of the Day.

Government bill   Legislative proposal by government; contrasted with private member bill in Westminster systems.

Incumbents   Members of legislature, especially those running for reelection.

Interest group   Private association that attempts to gain desired governmental action; *see* lobbyists.

Lobbyists   Persons, often paid professionals, who seek legislative and administrative action on behalf of themselves or clients; *see* interest group.

Matthew effect   Tendency of all election systems to provide extra share of seats to parties with the most votes.

Multimember district   Geographic area from which several members of parliament are elected; e.g., Sweden, Spain; *see* single-member district.

No confidence, vote of   Vote by parliament on continuance of a minister or whole government in office. German variation: constructive vote of no confidence.

Opposition parties   Parties in Parliament but not in government.

Override (of veto)   Legislative reconsideration of bill after executive veto.

Parliamentary system   Government is selected by, and can be dismissed by, Parliament; British origin; contrasted with dual-branch structure.

Party discipline   Requirement, and practice of, that legislative members vote with their parties.

Party list   Election ballots on which each party names its candidates in preferred order; the voter selects one party list.

Peak associations   Interest groups that are federations of many other and more specific groups; e.g., U.S. Chamber of Commerce.

Plurality election   Election system in which a parliamentary seat is allocated to the one candidate with the most votes in a district; Britain, Canada, the United States are examples; *see* proportional representation.

Private member bill   Legislative proposal introduced by a legislator; in Westminster systems, contrasted with government bill.

Proportional representation   Election system in which parliamentary seats are allocated in proportion to party share of vote in election; *see* plurality election.

Question time   Designated time for legislators orally to question government ministers; Westminster origin.

Roll call   Legislative voting in which members vote by name. Termed "division" in Britain.

Readings   Formal stages of procedure on the floor.

Second reading   Formal debate and voting prior to sending bill to committee in Westminster systems.

Select committees   Temporary and special-purpose committees; contrasted with standing committees; meaning differs between British and American practice (see appendix C).

Separation of powers   Independence of Congress and president from each other; dual-branch structure; American use; contrasted with parliamentary system.

Shadow cabinet   Leaders of opposition party who monitor policies and actions by government ministers; British.

Single-member district   Geographic area from which one member of parliament is elected; e.g., Britain, Canada, the United States; *see* multimember district.

Speaker   Presiding officer of the U.S. House of Representatives and of the House of Commons in Westminster systems.

Standing committees   Permanent committees; contrasted with select committees; meaning differs between British and American practice (see appendix C).

Three line whip   Whip notice with name of bill underlined three times; indicates vote of highest importance to party leaders; British. *See* whip notice.

Threshold   Minimum percentage of vote required for party to gain seats in parliament; e.g., 5 percent in Germany, 4 percent in Sweden.

Turnout, voter   Proportion of eligible electorate that votes in any one election.

Turnover   New legislative members in proportion to full membership.

Unicameral/ism   Parliaments with one chamber; contrasted with bicameralism; Sweden and Hungary are examples.

Veto   Formal disapproval of a bill by the chief executive.

Weimar Republic   German democratic political system in the 1920s between World War I and the rise of Adolf Hitler.

Westminster system   Parliaments based upon the British Parliament.

Whip   Party official in charge of attendance and voting by party members in legislature.

Whip notice   Memo to legislative party members from party whip about coming schedule (usually one week in advance) of legislation on floor. Westminster and U.S. term; *see* three line whip.

Appendix C

Congress and Parliament: American and British English

Phrase	American	British
Published floor debate	*Congressional Record*	*Hansard*
Second reading	Technical point of no substantive meaning	Major policy debate by which bill is accepted in principle
Standing committees	Most committees	Temporary bill committees
Select Committee	Special, temporary, few	Permanent departmental committees, and others
Government bill	Informally termed "Administration bill" introduced by member	Bills introduced by cabinet; privileged procedure
Private member bill	All bills	Nongovernment bills; few adopted
Ways and Means	Finance committee in House	House procedure for finance bills on floor

Phase	American	British
To limit debate	Cloture in Senate; rule in House	Guillotine; closure
To table	To stop debate	To initiate debate
Vote no confidence	—	Parliament vote on continuance of government
Government	"The administration"; president and immediate appointees	Prime minister, cabinet, ministers
Scrutiny	—	Review, criticism, debate of government bills, administration, actions, policy

References

Aberbach, Joel D.; Robert D. Putnam; and Bert A. Rockman. 1981. *Bureaucrats and Politicians in Western Democracies.* Cambridge, MA: Harvard.

Abraham, Henry J. 1986. *The Judicial Process: An Introductory Analysis of the Courts of the United States, England and France*, 5th ed. Oxford: Oxford University Press.

Abramowitz, Alan. 1991. "Incumbency, Campaign Spending, and the Decline of Competition in U.S. House Elections." *Journal of Politics, 53* (February): 34–56.

Ademolekan, Lapido. 1991. "Introduction: Federalism in Nigeria." *Publius, 21* (Fall): 1–11.

Agh, Attila. 1992. "The Emerging Party System in East Central Europe." *Budapest Papers on Democratic Transition*, no. 13. Budapest: Hungarian Center for Democracy Studies Foundation.

Arter, David. 1990. "The Swedish Riksdag: The Case of a Strong Policy-influencing Assembly." In Phillip Norton (ed.), *Parliaments in Western Europe.* London: Frank Cass, pp. 120–42.

Atkinson, Michael M., and David C. Docherty. 1992. "Moving Right Along: The Roots of Amaturism in the Canadian House of Commons." *Canadian Journal of Political Science, 25*, 2 (June): 295–318.

Baaklini, Abdo I., and A. Carlos Pojo do Rego. 1991. "Congress and the Development of a Computer Industry Policy in Brazil." In David M. Olson and Michael L. Mezey (eds.), *Legislatures in the Policy Process.* Cambridge: Cambridge University Press, pp. 130–59.

Bagehot, Walter. 1963. *The English Constitution.* Ithaca, NY: Cornell University Press.

Bailey, Sydney D. 1971. *British Parliamentary Democracy*, 3d ed. Boston: Houghton Mifflin.

Bates, St. John. 1988. "Scrutiny of Administration." In Michael Ryle and Peter G. Richards (eds.), *The Commons under Scrutiny.* London: Routledge, pp. 186–211.

Bean, Clive, and Anthony Mughan. 1989. "Leadership Effects in Parliamentary Elections in Australia and Britain." *American Political Science Review, 83* (December): 1165–80.

Belyaeva, Nina, and Vladimir Lipekhin. 1993. "Factions, Groups and Blocks in the Russian Parliament." *RFE/RL Research Report, 2*, 20 (May 14): 18–19.

Berglund, Sten, and Jan A. Dellenbrandt. 1992. "The Evolution of Party Systems in Eastern Europe." *Journal of Communist Studies, 8*, 1 (March): 148–59.

Berkman, Michael B. 1993. "Former State Legislators in the U.S. House of Representatives: Institutional and Policy Mastery." *Legislative Studies Quarterly, 18*, 1 (February): 77–104.

Bjurulf, Bo. 1972. "Froan Minoritetsparlamentarism till Majoritetskoalition." *Statsvetenskaplig Tidskrift, 2:* 125–88.

Blais, Andre. 1991. "The Debate over Electoral Systems." *International Political Science Review, 12*, 3 (July): 239–60.

Blondel, Jean. 1973. *Comparative Legislatures.* Englewood Cliffs, NJ: Prentice-Hall.

———. 1990. "The Government of France." In Michael Curtis (ed.), *Introduction to Comparative Government*, 2d ed. New York: Harper and Row.

Braunthal, Gerhard. 1972. *The West German Legislative Process: A Case Study of Two Transportation Bills.* Ithaca, NY: Cornell University Press.

Brokl, Lubomir. 1992. "Mezi listopadem 1989 a demokracii—antinomie nasi politiky." *Sociologicky United States Casopis, 28*, 2 (April): 150–64.

Burch, Martin, and Michael Moran. 1985. "The Changing British Political Elite, 1945–1983: MPs and Cabinet Ministers," *Parliamentary Affairs, 38*, 1 (Winter): 1–15.

Burda, Andrzej. 1978. *Parliament of the Polish People's Republic.* Warsaw: Ossolineum.

Butler, David, and Dennis Kavanagh. 1975. *The British General Election of October 1974.* New York: St. Martin's.

Campbell, Colin, and Ted Garrand. 1981. "Bureaucracy and Legislative Democracy in Canada, the U.K., the U.S. and Switzerland: From Turtle Syndrome to Collegiality." Prepared for the Annual Meeting of the American Political Science Association.

Campagna, Janet, and Bernard Grofman. 1990. "Party Control and Partisan Bias in 1980s Congressional Redistricting." *Journal of Politics, 52* (November): 1242–57.

Carroll, William A., and Norman B. Smith, eds. 1991. *American Constitutional Rights.* Lanham, MD: University Press of America.

Chressanthis, George; Kathie Gilbert; and Paul Grimes. 1991. "Ideology, Constituent Interests, and Senatorial Voting: The Case of Abortion." *Social Science Quarterly, 72*, 3 (September): 588–600.

Comisso, Ellen. 1992. "Federalism and Nationalism in Post-Socialist Eastern Europe." Paper read at the symposium, "Federalism for the New Europe," Cardozo School of Law, New York, September 10–12.

Cox, Gary W., and Maqthew D. McCubbins. 1991. "On the Decline of Party Voting in Congress." *Legislative Studies Quarterly, 16*, 4 (November): 547–70.

Cronin, Thomas. 1980. *The State of the Presidency*, 2d ed. Boston: Little, Brown.

Dalton, Russell J. 1989. *Politics in West Germany.* Glenview, IL: Scott, Foresman.

Damgaard, Erik, ed. 1992. *Parliamentary Change in the Nordic Countries.* Oslo: Scandinavian University Press.

Davidson, Roger. 1969. *The Role of the Congressman.* New York: Pegasus.

Davidson, Roger, and Walter Oleszek. 1990. *Congress and Its Members*, 3d. ed. Washington, DC: CQ Press.
————. 1994. *Congress and Its Members*, 4th ed. Washington, DC: CQ Press.
Drewry, Gavin. 1988. "Legislation." In Michael Ryle and Peter G. Richards (eds.), *The Commons under Scrutiny*. London: Routledge, pp. 120–40.
————, ed. 1989a. *The New Select Committees: A Study of the 1979 Reforms*. Oxford: Clarendon.
————. 1989b. "Scenes from Committee Life—The New Committees in Action." In Gavin Drewry (ed.), *The New Select Committees: A Study of the 1979 Reforms*. Oxford: Clarendon, pp. 348–66.
————. 1989c. "The 1979 Reforms—New Labels on Old Bottles?" In Gavin Drewry (ed.), *The New Select Committees: A Study of the 1979 Reforms*. Oxford: Clarendon, pp. 382–96.
————. 1989d. "The Committees since 1983." In Gavin Drewry (ed.), *The New Select Committees: A Study of the 1979 Reforms*. Oxford: Clarendon, pp. 397–53.
Dunleavy, Patrick, and Helen Margetts. 1992. "How Britain Would Have Voted under Alternative Electoral Systems in 1992." *Parliamentary Affairs, 45*, 4 (October): 640–55.
Eagles, Munroe. 1992. "The Political Ecology of Campaign Contributions in Canada: A Constituency-Level Analysis." *Canadian Journal of Political Science, 25* (September): 535–56.
Ehrmann, Henry W., and Martin A. Schain. 1992. *Politics in France*, 5th ed. New York: Harper Collins.
Elder, Neil; Alastair H. Thomas; and David Arter. 1982. *The Consensual Democracies?* Oxford: Martin Robertson.
Elster, Jon. 1991. "Constitutionalism in Eastern Europe: An Introduction." *University of Chicago Law Review, 58:* 447–82.
Epstein, Leon. 1967. *Political Parties in Western Democracy*. New York: Praeger.
Erickson, Lynda, and R.K. Carty. 1991. "Parties and Candidate Selection in the 1988 Canadian General Election." *Canadian Journal of Political Science, 24*, 2 (June): 331–49.
Fisher, Sharon. 1993. "Is Slovakia Headed for New Elections?" *RFE/RL Research Report* (August 13): 34–41.
Franklin, Daniel P. 1992. *Making Ends Meet*. Washington, DC: CQ Press.
Franklin, Charles H. 1993. "Senate Incumbent Visibility over the Election Cycle." *Legislative Studies Quarterly, 18*, 2 (May): 271–90.
Franks, C.E.S. 1987. *The Parliament of Canada*. Toronto: University of Toronto.
Franks, C.E.S., and David M. Olson. 1993. "Representation and the Policy Process in Federal Systems." In David M. Olson and C.E.S. Franks (eds.), *Representation and Policy Formation in Federal Systems*. Berkeley: University of California, Institute of Governmental Studies, pp. 2–31.
Frears, John. 1990. "The French Parliament: Loyal Workhorse, Poor Watchdog." In Phillip Norton (ed.), *Parliaments in Western Europe*. London: Frank Cass, pp. 32–51.
Gallagher, Michael. 1992. "Comparing Proportional Representation Electoral Systems: Quotas, Thresholds, Paradoxes, and Majorities." *British Journal of Political Science, 22*, 4 (October): 469–96.

Galloway, George. 1965. *History of the United States House of Representatives*. Washington, DC: House Committee on House Administration, House Doc. 250, 89th Congress.

Garton-Ash, Timothy. 1990. *The Magic Lantern*. New York: Random House.

Gebethner, Stanislaw, and Krzysztof Jasiewicz. 1993. *Political Data Yearbook, 1993: Poland*. Warsaw: Polish Academy of Sciences.

Gerlich, Peter. 1973. "The Institutionalization of European Paliaments." In Allan Kornberg (ed.), *Legislatures in Comparative Perspective*. New York: MacKay, pp. 94–113.

Giddings, Philip. 1989. "What Has Been Achieved?" In Gavin Drewry (ed.), *The New Select Committees: A Study of the 1979 Reforms*. Oxford: Clarendon, pp. 367–81.

Goldman, Stuart. 1991. "The New Soviet Legislative Branch." In Robert T. Huber and Donald R. Kelley (eds.), *Perestroika-Era Politics*. New York: M. E. Sharpe, pp. 51–78.

Gunther, Richard. 1989. "Electoral Laws, Party Systems, and Elites: The Case of Spain." *American Political Science Review, 83*, 3 (September): 835–58.

Gwertzman, Bernard, and Michael T. Kaufman, eds. 1990. *The Collapse of Communism*. New York: New York Times Books/Random House.

Hammond, Susan W. 1991. "Congressional Caucuses and Party Leaders in the House of Representative." *Political Science Quarterly, 106* (Summer): 277–94.

Hancock, M. Donald. 1972. *Sweden: The Politics of Postindustrial Change*. Hinsdale, IL: Dryden.

———. 1993. "Sweden." In M. Donald Hancock (ed.), *Politics in Western Europe*. Chatam, NJ: Chatam House.

Hansard Society Committee on the Legislative Process. 1992. *Making the Law: The Report*. London: The Hansard Society for Parliamentary Government.

Harrison, John B., and Richard E. Sullivan. 1980. *A Short History of Western Civilization*, 5th ed. New York: Knopf.

Heclo, Hugh. 1978. "Issue Networks and the Executive Establishment." In Anthony King (ed.), *The New American Political System*. Washington, DC: AEI.

Heidenheimer, Arnold J.; Hugh Heclo; and Carolyn T. Adams. 1990. *Comparative Public Policy*, 3d ed. New York: St. Martin's.

Hibbing, John, and Ivan Volgyes. 1992. "Political Elite Composition in the Wake of a Peaceful Revolution: Hungary 1990." Paper presented to Southern Political Science Association, Atlanta.

Hough, Jerry. 1989. "The Politics of Successful Economic Reform." *Soviet Economy, 5*, 1: 3–46.

Huber, Robert T., and Donald R. Kelley, eds. 1991. *Perestroika-Era Politics*. New York: M. E. Sharpe.

Irwin, Helen. 1988. "Opportunities for Backbenchers." In Michael Ryle and Peter G. Richards (eds.), *The Commons under Scrutiny*. London: Routledge, pp. 76–98.

Isberg, Magnus. 1982. *The First Decade of the Unicameral Riksdag: The Role of the Swedish Parliament in the 1970's*. Stockholm: Statsvetenskapliga institutionen, Stockholms Universitet.

Jacobson, Gary C. 1991. "The Persistence of Democratic House Majorities." In Gary W. Cox and Samuel Kernell (eds.), *The Politics of Divided Government.* Boulder, CO: Westview.

Jain, R.B. 1991. "Electronics Policy and the Indian Parliament." In David M. Olson and Michael L. Mezey (eds.), *Legislatures in the Policy Process.* Cambridge: Cambridge University Press.

Jasiewicz, Krzysztof. 1993. "Polish Politics on the Eve of the 1993 Elections: Toward Fragmentation or Pluralism?" *Communist and Post-Communist Studies, 26,* 4 (December).

Jogerst, Michael. 1993. *Reform in the House of Commons: The Select Committee System.* Lexington, KY: University of Kentucky Press.

Johnson, Nevil. 1988. "Departmental Select Committees." In Michael Ryle and Peter G. Richards (eds.), *The Commons under Scrutiny.* London: Routledge, pp. 157–85.

Kenny, Christopher, and Michael McBurnett. 1992. "A Dynamic Model of the Effect of Campaign Spending on Congressional Vote Choice." *American Journal of Political Science, 36* (November): 923–37.

King, Anthony. 1976. "Models of Executive–Legislative Relations: Great Britain, France, and West Germany." *Legislative Studies Quarterly, 1,* 1 (February): 11–36.

King, Gary, and Andrew Gelman. 1991. "Systemic Consequences of Incumbency Advantage in U.S. House Elections." *American Journal of Political Science, 35* (February): 110–38.

Kingdon, John W. 1984. *Agenda, Alternatives, and Public Policies.* Boston: Little, Brown.

Kirchheimer, Otto. 1966. "The Transformation of the Western European Party System." In Joseph LaPalombara and Myron Weiner (eds.), *Political Parties and Political Development.* Princeton, NJ: Princeton University Press, pp. 177–200.

Korosenyi, Andras. 1991. "Revival of the Past or New Beginning? The Nature of Post-Communist Politics." In Gyorgy Szoboszlai (ed.), *Democracy and Political Transformation.* Budapest: Hungarian Political Science Association.

Kurland, Philip, and Ralph Lerner, eds. 1987. *The Founders' Constitution,* vol 1. Chicago: University of Chicago Press.

LaPalombara, Joseph, and Myron Weiner. 1966. "The Origin and Development of Political Parties." In Joseph LaPalombara and Myron Weiner (eds.), *Political Parties and Political Development.* Princeton: Princeton University, pp. 3–42.

Laundy, Philip. 1979. "The Speaker and His Office in the Twentieth Century." In S.A. Walkland (ed.), *The House of Commons in the Twentieth Century.* Oxford: Clarendon, pp. 124–203.

Laumann, Edward O., and David Knoke. 1987. *The Organizational State.* Madison: University of Wisconsin Press.

Lees, John D., and Malcolm Shaw, eds. 1979. *Committees in Legislatures: A Comparative Analysis.* Durham, NC: Duke University Press.

LeLoup, Lance T., and Steven A. Shull. 1993. *Congress and the President: The Policy Connection.* Belmont, CA: Wadsworth.

LeLoup, Lance T., and John T. Woolley. 1991. "Legislative Oversight of Monetary Policy in France, Germany, Great Britain, and the United States." In

David M. Olson and Michael L. Mezey (eds.), *Legislatures in the Policy Process*. Cambridge: Cambridge University Press, pp. 25–58.

Lewis-Beck, Michael S. 1988. *Economics and Elections*. Ann Arbor: University of Michigan Press.

Liebert, Ulrike, and Maurizio Cotta, eds. 1990. *Parliament and Democratic Consolidation in Southern Europe*. London: Pinter.

Lijphart, Arend. 1984. *Democracies: Patterns of Majoritarian and Consensus Government in Twenty-One Countries*. New Haven: Yale University Press.

———. 1986. "Proportionality by Non-PR Methods: Ethnic Representation in Belgium, Cyprus, Lebanon, New Zealand, West Germany and Zimbabwe." In Bernard Grofman and Arend Lijphart (eds.), *Electoral Laws and Their Political Consequences*. New York: Agathon, 1986.

———. 1990. "The Political Consequences of Electoral Laws, 1945–85." *American Political Science Review, 84*, 2 (June): 481–96.

Linz, Juan, and Alfred Stepan. 1992. "Political Identities and Electoral Sequences: Spain, the Soviet Union, and Yugoslavia." *Daedalus* (Spring): 123–139.

Loewenberg, Gerhard. 1967. *Parliament in the German Political System*. Ithaca, NY: Cornell University Press.

———. 1993. "The New Political Leadership of Central Europe: The Example of the Hungarian National Assembly." Paper for the conference, "Comparative Parliamentary Development in Eastern Europe and the Former USSR," Emory University, April, Atlanta.

Loewenberg, Gerhard, and Samuel C. Patterson. 1979. *Comparing Legislatures*. Boston: Little, Brown.

Longley, Lawrence D. 1988. "The Politics of Electoral Reform in the UK and USA." *Parliamentary Affairs, 41* (October): 527–35.

McGregor, James. 1993. "How Electoral Laws Shape Eastern Europe's Parliaments." *RFE/RL Research Report, 2*, 4 (January 22): 11–18.

Mainwaring, Scott. 1991. "Politicans, Parties, and Electoral Systems: Brazil and Comparative Perspective." *Comparative Politics, 24*, 1 (October): 21–43.

Mamadough, V.C., and H.H. Van Der Wusten. 1989. "The Influence of the Change of Electoral System on Political Representation: The Case of France in 1985." *Political Geography Quarterly, 8*, 2 (April): 145–59.

Marongiu, Antonio. 1968. *Medieval Parliaments: A Comparative Study*. London: Eyre and Spottiswoode.

Mason, David S. 1991. "The Polish Parliament and Labor Legislation During Solidarity." In David M. Olson and Michael L. Mezey (eds.), *Legislatures in the Policy Process*. Cambridge: Cambridge University Press, pp. 179–200.

"The Media in Eastern Europe." 1993. *RFE/RL Research Report, 2*, 19 (May 7): 22–35.

Mezey, Michael L. 1979. *Comparative Legislatures*. Durham, NC: Duke University Press.

———. 1991. "Parliaments and Public Policy: An Assessment." In David M. Olson and Michael L. Mezey (eds.), *Legislatures in the Policy Process*. Cambridge: Cambridge University Press, pp. 201–14.

Moe, Ronald C., and Steven C. Teel. 1970. "Congress as Policy-Maker: A Necessary Reappraisal." *Political Science Quarterly* (September): 443–70.

Mueller, Wolfgang. 1992. "The Catch-all Party Thesis and the Austrian Social Democrats." *German Politics, 1*, 2 (August): 181–99.

Mueller-Rommel, Ferdinand. 1990. "Interest Group Representation in the Bundestag." In Uwe Thaysen, Roger Davidson, and Robert G. Livingston (eds.), *The U.S. Congress and the German Bundestag.* Boulder, CO: Westview Press, pp. 313–340.

Mughan, Anthony. 1990. "Midterm Popularity and Governing Party Dissension in the House of Commons, 1959–79." *Legislative Studies Quarterly, 15* (August): 341–56.

Neumann, Sigmund. 1956. "Germany: Changing Patterns and Lasting Problems." In Sigmund Neumann (ed.), *Modern Political Parties.* Chicago: University of Chicago Press.

Norris, Pippa. 1987. *Politics and Sexual Equality: The Comparative Position of Women in Western Democracies.* Boulder, CO: Rienner.

Norris, Pippa; Elizabeth Vallance; and Joni Lovenduski. 1992. "Do Candidates Make a Difference? Gender, Race, Ideology and Incumbency." *Parliamentary Affairs, 45*, 4 (October): 496–517.

Norton, Phillip. 1979. "The Organization of Parliamentary Parties." In S.A. Walkland (ed.), *The House of Commons in the Twentieth Century.* Oxford: Clarendon, pp. 7–68.

———. 1981. *The Commons in Perspective.* New York: Longman.

———. 1988. "Opposition to Government." In Michael Ryle and Peter G. Richards (eds.), *The Commons under Scrutiny.* London: Routledge, pp. 99–119.

———, ed. 1990. *Parliaments in Western Europe.* London: Frank Cass.

———. 1991. *The British Polity,* 2d ed. New York: Longman.

———. 1993. "Independence without Entrenchment: The British House of Commons in the Post-Thatcher Era." Paper presented to American Political Science Association, Washington, DC, September 2–5.

Offe, Claus. 1991. "Capitalism by Democratic Design? Democratic Theory Facting the Triple Transition in East Central Europe." *Social Research, 58*, 4 (Winter): 865–92.

Oleszek, Walter J. 1978. *Congressional Procedures and the Policy Process.* Washington, DC: CQ Press.

Olson, David M. 1980. *The Legislative Process: A Comparative Approach.* New York: Harper and Row.

———. 1993a. "Compartmentalized Competition: The Managed Transitional Election System of Poland." *Journal of Politics, 55*, 2 (May): 415–441.

———. 1993b. "Dissolution of the State: Political Parties and the 1992 Election in Czechoslovakia." *Communist and Post Communist Studies, 26*, 3 (September): 299–312.

Olson, David M.; Roger Davidson; and Thomas Klephart. 1991. "Industrial Policy Agenda and Options in Congress and the Executive in the United States." In David M. Olson and Michael L. Mezey (eds.), *Legislatures in the Policy Process.* Cambridge: Cambridge University Press, pp. 81–102.

Olson, David M., and C.E.S. Franks, eds. 1993. *Representation and Policy Formation in Federal Systems.* Berkeley: University of California, Institute of Governmental Studies.

Olson, David M., and Ian Fried. 1992. "Party and Party System in Regime Transformation: The Inner Transition in Poland and Czechoslovakia." Paper read at American Political Science Association, Chicago.

Olson, David M., and Michael L. Mezey, eds. 1991a. *Legislatures in the Policy Process.* Cambridge: Cambridge University Press.

————. 1991b. "Parliaments and Public Policy." In David M. Olson and Michael L. Mezey, (eds.), *Legislatures in the Policy Process.* Cambridge: Cambridge University Press, pp. 1–24.

Olson, David M.; J. Pierre; and R. Piotrowski. 1983. "Documentary Data in the Comparison of Committee Systems in National Parliaments: Riksdagen and the Polish Sejm." *Statsvetenskaplig Tidskrift, 3:* 356–66.

Olson, David M., and Maurice D. Simon. 1986. "The Institutional Development of a Minimal Parliament: The Case of the Polish Sejm." In Stephen White and Daniel Nelson (eds.), *Communist Politics.* London: Macmillan, and New York: New York University Press.

Olson, David M.; Jindriska Syllova; and Jana Reschova. 1993. "Prvni volebni obdobi demokratickeho parlamentu v CSFR: Federalni shromazdeni 1990–92: komparacni pohled" (The First Term of the Democratic Parliament of the Czech and Slovak Federal Republic: A Comparative Perspective). *Pravnik 132,* 2: 125–41.

Orfield, Gary. 1975. *Congressional Power: Congress and Social Change.* New York: Harcourt, Brace, Jovanovich.

Ornstein, Norman, ed. 1981. *The Role of the Legislature in Western Democracies.* Washington, DC: AEI

————. 1990. "Interest Representation in the Capitol." In Uwe Thaysen, Roger Davidson, and Robert G. Livingston (eds.), *The U.S. Congress and the German Bundestag.* Boulder, CO: Westview Press, pp. 297–312.

Ost, David. 1990. *Solidarity and the Politics of Anti-Politics.* Philadelphia: Temple University Press.

Pacek, Alexander. 1992. "New Political Parties in Eastern Europe: Building a Research Agenda." *VOX POP Newsletter, 10,* 3: 1, 5, 7–8.

Pehe, Jiri. 1993. "Constitutional Imbroglio in the Czech Republic." *RFE-RL Research Report, 2* (January 29).

Peters, B. Guy. 1991. *European Politics Reconsidered.* New York: Holmes and Meier.

Pitkin, Hannah. 1967. *The Concept of Representation.* Berkeley: University of California Press.

Polsby, Nelson W. 1968. "The Institutionalization of the House of Representatives." *American Political Science Review, 62* (March): 144–68.

Poulard, Jean V. 1990. "The French Double Executive and the Experience of Cohabitation." *Political Science Quarterly, 105,* 2 (Summer): 243–67.

Ranney, Austin. 1965. *Pathways to Parliament.* Madison: University of Wisconsin Press.

Remmington, Thomas F. 1991. "Parliamentary Government in the USSR." In Robert T. Huber and Donald R. Kelley (eds.), *Perestroika-Era Politics.* New York: M. E. Sharpe, pp. 175–204.

Remington, Thomas; Steven S. Smith; and D. Roderick Kiewiet. 1993. "Voting Alignments in the Russian Copngress of Peoples Deputies." Paper for Conference on Comparative Parliamentary Development, Emory University, Atlanta, April 9–10.

Reschova, Jana. 1992. "Nova politika s novymi ludmi: Federalne zhromzdenie v roku 1990." *Sociologicky Casopis, 28,* 2 (Duben): 222–36.

Richards, Peter G. 1979. "Private Members' Legislation." In S.A. Walkland (ed.), *The House of Commons in the Twentieth Century.* Oxford: Clarendon, pp. 292–328.

Ripley, Randall. 1983. *Congress: Process and Policy,* 3d ed. New York: W.W. Norton.

Ripley, Randall, and Grace A. Franklin. 1991. *Congress, the Bureaucracy and Public Policy,* 5th ed. Pacific Grove, CA: Brooks/Cole.

Robinson, Ann. 1988. "The House of Commons and Public Money." In Michael Ryle and Peter G. Richards (eds.), *The Commons under Scrutiny.* London: Routledge, pp. 141–56.

Rona-Tas, Akos. 1991. "The Selected and the Elected: The Making of the New Parliamentary Elite in Hungary." *East European Politics and Societies, 5,* 3 (Fall): 357–93.

Rose, Richard. 1991. *The Postmodern President,* 2d ed. Chatam, NJ: Chatam House.

Russell, Conrad. 1979. *Parliaments and English Politics 1621–1629.* Oxford: Clarendon Press.

Ryle, Michael. 1988. "Where Have We Got To?" In Michael Ryle and Peter G. Richards (eds.), *The Commons under Scrutiny.* London: Routledge, pp. 229–41.

Ryle, Michael, and Peter G. Richards, eds. 1988. *The Commons under Scrutiny.* London: Routledge.

Saalfeld, Thomas. 1990. "The West Germany Bundestag after 40 Years." In Phillip Norton (ed.), *Parliaments in Western Europe.* London: Frank Cass, pp. 68–89.

Sabato, Larry J. 1985. *PAC Power.* New York: Norton

Sanction, Andrew. 1990. "Eroding Representation-by-Population in the Canadian House of Commons: The Representation Act, 1985." *Canadian Journal of Political Science, 23* (September): 441–57.

Sanford, George. 1992. "The Polish Road to Democratisation: From Political Impasse to the 'Controlled Abdication' of Communist Power." In George Sanford (ed.), *Democratization in Poland, 1988–90.* New York: St. Martin's Press, pp. 1–34.

Sassoon, Donald. 1986. *Contemporary Italy.* New York: Longman.

Schlesinger, Arthur. 1992. "Leave the Constitution Alone." In Arend Lijphart (ed.), *Parliamentary versus Presidential Government.* Oxford: Oxford University Press, pp. 90–94.

Schlesinger, Joseph A., and Mildred Schlesinger. 1990. "The Reaffirmation of a Multiparty System in France." *American Political Science Review, 84,* 4 (December): 1077–1102.

Schwarz, John E., and L. Earl Shaw. 1976. *The United States Congress in Comparative Perspective.* Hinsdale, IL: Dryden.

Searing, Donald D. 1987. "New Roles for Postwar British Politics: Ideologues, Generalists, Specialists and the Progress of Professionalization in Parliament." *Comparative Politics, 19,* 4 (July): 431–52.

Seligman, Lee. 1979. "A Reassessment of the Two Presidencies Thesis." *Journal of Politics, 41* (November): 1195–1205.

Shaffer, William. 1991. "Interparty Spatial Relationships in Norwegian Storting Roll-Call Votes." *Scandinavian Political Studies, 14*, 1: 59–80.

Shaw, Malcolm. 1979. "Conclusion." In John D. Lees and Malcolm Shaw (eds.), *Committees in Legislatures: A Comparative Analysis.* Durham, NC: Duke University Press.

Shugart, Matthew S. 1992. "Electoral Reform in Systems of Proportional Representation." *European Journal of Political Science, 21*, 3 (April): 207–24.

Shugart, Matthew S., and John M. Carey. 1992. *Presidents and Assemblies: Constitutional Design and Electoral Dynamics.* Cambridge: Cambridge University Press.

Simon, Janos. 1993a. "Post-paternalist Political Culture in Hungary: Relationship between Citizens and Politics during and after the 'Melancholic Revolution' (1989–1991)." *Communist and Post-Communist Studies, 26*, 2 (June): 226–38.

———. 1993b. *Fieldmarshal's Baton and Peace.* Budapest: Academy of Science.

Skala, Josef, and Christoph Kunkel. 1992. "Auf dem Weg zu einem konsolidierten Parteiensystem?" *Geschichte und Gesellschaft, 18*, 3: 292–308.

Smith, Stephen S., and Christopher J. Deering. 1984. *Committees in Congress.* Washington, DC: CQ Press.

Sorauf, Frank. 1980. *Party Politics in America*, 4th ed. Boston: Little, Brown.

Sorauf, Frank J. 1988. *Money in American Elections.* Glenview, IL: Scott Foresman.

Squire, Peverill. 1991. "Preemptive Fund-Raising and Challenger Profile in Senate Elections." *Journal of Politics, 53* (November): 1150–64.

———. 1992. "Challenger Quality and Voting Behavior in U.S. Senate Elections." *Legislative Studies Quarterly, 17* (May): 247–64.

Steffani, Winfried. 1990. "Parties (Parliamentary Groups) and Committees in the Bundestag." In Uwe Thaysen, Roger Davidson, and Robert G. Livingston (eds.), *The U.S. Congress and the German Bundestag.* Boulder, CO: Westview Press, pp. 273–96.

Steiner, Juerg. 1991. *European Democracies*, 2d ed. New York: Longman.

Stewart, Ian. 1993. "No Quick Fixes: The Canadian Central Government and the Problems of Representation." In David M. Olson and C.E.S. Franks (eds.), *Representation and Policy Formation in Federal Systems.* Berkeley: University of California, Institute of Governmental Studies, pp. 33–74.

Stjernquist, Nils, and Bo Bjurulf. 1970. "Party Cohesion and Party Cooperation in the Swedish Parliament in 1964 and 1966." *Scandinavian Political Studies, 5:* 129–64.

Syllova, Jindriska. 1992. "Ceska narodni rada v roce 1990: Analyza slozeni a cinnosti." *Sociologicky Casopis, 28*, 2 (Duben): 237–46.

Taagepera, Rein, and Matthew S. Shugart. 1993. "Predicting the Number of Parties: A Quantitataive Model of Duverger's Mechanical Effect." *American Political Science Review, 87* (June): 455–64.

Truman, David. 1951. *The Governmental Process.* New York: Knopf.

Tucker, Robert C., ed. 1975. *The Lenin Anthology.* New York: Norton.

Vachudova, Milada A. 1993. "Divisions in the Czech Communist Party." *RFE/RL Research Report, 2*, 37 (September 17): 28–33.

Vinton, Louisa. 1993. "Poland's Political Spectrum on the Eve of the Elections." *RFE/RL Research Report, 2*, 36 (September 10): 1–16.

von Beyme, Klaus. 1990. "Economic and Social Policy in the Bundestag." In Uwe Thaysen, Roger Davidson, and Robert G. Livingston (eds.), *The U.S. Congress and the German Bundestag*. Boulder, CO: Westview Press, pp. 367–80.

Walkland, S.A. 1979a. "Government Legislation in the House of Commons." In S.A. Walkland (ed.), *The House of Commons in the Twentieth Century*. Oxford: Clarendon, pp. 247–91.

———, ed. 1979b. *The House of Commons in the Twentieth Century*. Oxford: Clarendon.

Watts, Ronald. 1993. "Representation in the North American Federations: A Comparative Perspective." In David M. Olson and C.E.S. Franks (eds.), *Representation and Policy Formation in Federal Systems*. Berkeley: University of California, Institute of Governmental Studies, pp. 291–321.

Wayne, Stephen J. 1978. *The Legislative Presidency*. New York: Harper and Row.

Wesolowski, Wlodzimierz. 1990. "Transition from Authoritarianism to Democracy." *Social Research, 57* (Summer): 435–61.

White, Stephen, and Gordon Wightman. 1989. "Gorbachev's Reforms: The Soviet Elections of 1989." *Parliamentary Affairs, 42:* 560–81.

Williamson, James A. 1931. *The Evolution of England: A Commentary on the Facts*. Oxford: Clarendon.

Wilson, Frank L. 1989. "Evolution of the French Party System." In Paul Godt (ed.), *Policy-Making in France: From de Gaulle to Mitterand*. London: Pinter.

Wilson, Woodrow. 1956. *Congressional Government*. New York: Meridian Books (originally published 1885).

Wood, David M. 1991. "The British House of Commons and Industrial Policy." In David M. Olson and Michael L. Mezey (eds.), *Legislatures in the Policy Process*. Cambridge: Cambridge University Press, pp. 103–29.

Wood, David M., and Phillip Norton. 1992. "Do Candidates Matter? Constituency-Specific Vote Change for Incumbent MPs, 1983–87." *Political Studies, 40,* 2 (June): 227–38.

Woshinsky, Oliver H. 1973. *The French Deputy: Incentives and Behavior in the National Assembly*. Lexington, MA: Lexington Books.

Zakrzewski, Witold. 1982. "Die gesetzgeberische Taetigkeit des Parlaments (Sejm) der Volksrepublik Polen in der VIII Legislaturperiode bis 13. December 1981." *Ost-Europa Rechts*, 3/4: 210–41.

Ziegler, L. Harmon. 1993. *Political Parties in Industrial Democracies*. Itasca, IL: Peacock.

Author Index

Aberbach, Joel D., 27
Abraham, Henry J., 92
Abramowitz, Alan, 108
Adamolekan, Lapido, 33
Agh, Attila, 115
Arter, David, 68, 82, 87
Atkinson, Michael M., 17, 30

Baaklini, Abdo I., 135, 136, 143
Bagehot, Walter, 2
Bailey, Sydney, 2, 20, 42, 112
Bates, St. John, 60, 65
Bean, Clive, 103
Belyaeva, Nina, 129
Berglund, Sten, 123
Berkman, Michael B., 16
Bjurulf, Bo, 51
Blais, Andre, 95
Blondel, Jean, 7, 79, 91
Braunthal, Gerhard, 134
Brokl, Lubomir, 121
Burch, Martin, 21, 24
Burda, Andrzej, 137
Butler, David, 25

Campagna, Janet, 105
Campbell, Colin, 134
Carey, John M., 79, 95
Carroll, William A., 4
Carty, R.K., 101
Chressanthis, George, 27
Comisso, Ellen, 124

Cotta, Maurizio, 115
Cox, Gary W., 50
Cronin, Thomas, 67

Dalton, Russell, 18, 21, 22, 23, 25, 26,
    35, 107, 109, 134
Damgaard, Erik, 36, 82, 142
Davidson, Roger, 19, 28, 87, 103, 107,
    110, 112
Deering, Christopher J., 71, 120
Dellenbrandt, Jan A., 123
Docherty, David C., 17, 30
Drewry, Gavin, 59, 60, 64, 72, 89
Dunleavy, Patrick, 97

Eagles, Munroe, 108
Ehrmann, Henry W., 33, 36, 59, 85,
    140, 142
Elder, Neil, 36
Elster, Jon, 127
Epstein, Leon, 50, 54, 101
Erickson, Lynda, 101

Fisher, Sharon, 123
Franklin, Charles H., 105
Franklin, Daniel P., 64, 91
Franklin, Grace, 109, 140
Franks, C.E.S., 24, 26, 41, 51, 71, 89, 91
Frears, John, 24, 85

Gallagher, Michael, 95
Galloway, George, 116

Garrand, Ted, 134
Garton-Ash, Timothy, 118, 121
Gebethner, Stanislaw, 125, 127
Gelman, Andrew, 105
Gerlich, Peter, 112
Gewertzman, Bernard, 118
Giddings, Philip, 61
Goldman, Stuart, 129
Grofman, Bernard, 105
Gunther, Richard, 124

Hammond, Susan W., 48
Hancock, M. Donald, 24, 36
Harrison, John B., 39
Heclo, Hugh, 108
Heidenheimer, Arnold J., 110
Hibbing, John, 119
Hough, Jerry, 129

Irwin, Helen, 91
Isberg, Magnus, 47, 50, 134, 135, 138

Jacobson, Gary C., 105
Jain, R.B., 91
Jasiewicz, Krzysztof, 122, 125, 127
Jogerst, Michael, 14, 17, 18, 29, 58, 71
Johnson, Nevil, 65, 143

Kaufman, Michael T., 118
Kavanagh, Dennis, 25
Kenny, Christopher, 108
King, Anthony, 7
King, Gary, 105
Kingdon, John W., 88
Kirchheimer Otto, 38
Knoke, David, 109
Korosenyi, Andras, 116
Kunkel, Christoph, 121
Kurland, Philip, 2

LaPolombara, Joseph, 38
Laumann, Edward O., 109
Laundy, Philip, 9, 41
Lees, James D., 139
LeLoup, Lance T., 47, 88, 135, 136, 138
Lerner, Ralph, 2
Lewis-Beck, Michael, 38
Liebert, Ulrike, 115

Lijphart, Arend, 23, 25, 78, 79, 82
Linz, Juan, 124
Lipekhin, Vladimir, 129
Loewenberg, Gerhard, 4, 7, 9, 20, 42,
    47, 84, 119, 138
Longley, Lawrence D., 113

Mainwaring, Scott, 101,
Mamadough, V.C., 95
Margetts, Helen, 97
Marongiu, Antonio, 4
Mason, David S., 124, 143
McBurnett, Michael, 108
McCubbins, Mathew D., 50
McGregor, James, 124
Mezey, Michael L., 7, 54, 132, 133,
    139
Moe, Ronald C., 143
Moran, Michael, 21, 24
Mueller, Wolfgang, 39
Mueller-Rommel, Ferdinand, 25, 109
Mughan, Anthony, 51, 105

Neumann, Sigmund, 33
Norris, Pippa, 23, 105
Norton, Philip, 9, 25, 43, 46, 47, 48,
    50, 77, 101, 105, 109, 110, 113,
    134, 143

Offe, Claus, 116
Oleszek, Walter, 28, 87, 103, 107,
    110, 112, 120
Olson, David M., 16, 24, 47, 65, 91,
    92, 120, 121, 122, 123, 124, 132,
    133, 134, 139, 140, 143
Orfield, Gary, 143
Ornstein, Norman, 28, 109
Ost, David, 118, 122

Pacek, Alexander, 123
Patterson, Samuel C., 7, 9, 20, 22, 26,
    28, 84
Pehe, Jiri, 123, 127
Peters, B. Guy, 37, 61, 84, 99, 103,
    110
Pierre, Jon, 16
Piotrowski, R., 16
Pitkin, Hannah, 4

Pojo do Rego, A. Carlos, 135, 136, 143
Polsby, Nelson, 17
Poulard, Jean V., 80

Ranney, Austin, 101
Remington, Thomas F., 129
Reschova, Jana, 199
Richards, Peter G., 85
Ripley, Randall, 53, 109, 140
Robinson, Ann, 64
Rona-Tas, Akos, 21, 116
Rose, Richard, 83
Russell, Conrad, 14, 20
Ryle, Michael, 29, 41, 85

Saalfeld, Thomas, 50, 51
Sabato, Larry J., 107
Sanction, Andrew, 105
Sanford, George, 118
Sassoon, Donald, 35
Schain, Martin A., 33, 36, 59, 85, 140, 142
Schlesinger, Arthur, 79
Schlesinger, Joseph A., 95
Schlesinger, Mildred, 95
Schwarz, John E., 64, 84, 85
Searing, Donald D., 18, 47
Seligman, Lee, 50
Shaffer, William, 51
Shaw, Malcolm, 59, 139
Shaw L. Earl, 64, 84, 85
Shugart, Matthew S., 79, 95
Shull, Steven A., 88
Simon, Janos, 116, 128
Simon, Maurice, 91, 124, 143
Skala, Josef, 121
Smith, Norman B., 4
Smith, Stephen S., 71, 120
Sorauf, Frank, 101, 108

Squire, Peverill, 105, 108
Steffani, Winfried, 3, 59, 64, 70, 88, 140
Steiner, Juerg, 82, 95, 103, 137
Stepan, Alfred, 124
Stewart, Ian, 24, 51
Stjernquist, Nils, 51
Sullivan, Richard E., 39
Syllova, Jindriska, 119

Taagepera, Rein, 95
Teel, Steven C., 143
Thaysen, Uwe, 83
Thomas, Alastair H., 36
Truman, David, 108, 135
Tucker, Robert C., 57

Vachudova, Milada A., 123
Van Der Wusten, H.H., 95
Vinton, Louisa, 123
von Beyme, Klaus, 85
Volgyes, Ivan, 119

Walkland, S.A., 57, 86, 88
Watts, Ronald, 26, 113
Wayne, Stephen J., 88
Weiner, Myron, 38
Wesolowski, Wlodzimierz, 116
White, Stephen, 129
Wightman, Gordon, 129
Williamson, James A., 4
Wilson, Frank L., 36
Wilson, Woodrow, 57
Wood, David M., 105, 135
Woolley, John T., 47, 135, 136, 138
Woshinsky, Oliver H., 19

Zakrzewski, Witold, 124
Ziegler, L. Harmon, 95, 101, 110

Subject Index

Activity in policy, factors, 132–33
Administrative structure, 133, 134–35, 138
American Congress. *See* U.S. Congress
Appropriations, 2, 61, 64, 89–91
Australia, 103
Austria, 38, 103, 109
Authoritarian legislatures, 9, 54, 105, 143

Back bench, 18, 29, 43–46
Baird, Zoe, 92
Baker v. *Carr* (U.S.), 112
Baltic states, 129
Belgium, 33, 126
Bentsen, Lloyd, secretary of the treasury, 76
Bicameralism
  coordination committees, 70–71, 150
  mediation committee (Germany), 89
  members, 25–26
  number, 25
  postcommunist countries, 126
  Russian Republic, 129
  split party control, 71
Bills
  government, 50, 84
  introduction, 147
  prelegislative stages, 87, 142
  private member, 85, 147
  readings, 146, 148
Bismarck, Otto von, 9

Bonner, Jack, 16
Boothroyd, Betty, Speaker, 41
Bork, Robert, 92
Brazil, 101, 135, 136, 143, 144
Britain
  budget, 61–64, 89
  committees, 28, 43, 57–58, 71–72, 85–86, 139, 143, 148
  Conservative 1922 Committee, 48
  documents, 68, 69
  elections, 34, 95, 96, 97–98, 99, 101, 102, 106, 112, 135
  Euro-sceptics, Conservative Party, 52, 77–78
  floor, 42, 66–67
    seating, 39–41
  Glorious Revolution, 14
  government, 58–59, 65, 76–78, 84–85, 86, 139, 143, 147
    bills, 50
    Labour, minority, 51
    legislation criticized, 89
  House of Lords, 25–26
  interest groups, 88, 109, 112
  legislative stages, 146
  members, 13, 17–18, 20, 21, 22, 23, 24, 28–29, 141
    sponsored, 24–25
  opposition party, 43, 89
  Parliament
    early, 4, 6, 14, 20, 42
    Labour Party, 48

Britain *(continued)*
parties, 43–46, 47, 48, 137, 139
party voting, 50–51
policy advocate roles, 18
prime minister selection, 43–44
private member, 85, 86, 147
rebellion, 50
second reading, 59, 67, 148
shadow cabinet, 44
whip, 46
white paper, 87, 147
Bulgaria, 127
Bush, George, president, 52, 86, 90

Cabinet. *See* Government
Callaghan, James, prime minister, 79
Campaigns, election. *See* Elections
Campbell, Ben Nighthorse, senator, 16
Campbell, Kim, prime minister, 44, 83
Canada, 27, 34, 44, 48, 68, 69
committees, 71–72, 139
confidence votes, 51
elections, 95–98, 99, 102, 105, 106, 108, 112–13
members lack provincial experience, 24
prime minister selection, 82
Senate, appointive, 26
tenure, 17
Candidates for election. *See* Elections
Carter, Jimmy, president, 88
Central Europe, 66, 70, 109
See also Postcommunist legislatures
Chief executive
legislative independence from, 7, 12, 42, 43, 73, 74, 76–78, 86, 134, 143
legislature, interaction with, 7, 12, 74
selection, 82–83
Churchill, Sir Winston, 39, 41, 79
Clinton, Bill, president, 27–28, 47, 76, 88, 107, 111
Committees; by name
Appropriations (United States), 64
Appropriations (Germany), 64
Foreign Relations (U.S. Senate), 61
Government Operations (United States), 60

Committees; by name *(continued)*
Finance (U.S. Senate), 90
Law and Legislation (Central Europe), 70
Mediation (Germany), 70
Public Accounts (Britain), 60, 65
Trade and Industry (Britain), 60 62–3
Treasury and Civil Service (Britain), 61
Watergate (U.S. Senate), 60
Ways and Means (U.S. House of Representatives), 90
Committees, chamber
ad hoc committees, 57–58
administrative agencies, parallel to, 56, 139
administrative review, 60, 91, 140, 143
amendments, 58–59, 85
appropriations, 61, 63, 90
bill committee, 57, 139, 148
chairpersons, 43, 56, 65, 72
constitutional stipulations, 140
coordination, 70
departmental, 58, 71
documents, 67–69
experience compared with cabinet, 57, 141
floor and, 66
government, 57, 65, 67
hearings, 68
jurisdiction, 140
legislation, 60
member satisfaction, 28–29
member selection, 42, 64–65
models, U.S.-British contrast, 57–58
party
compared with, 137–38, 140
discipline, 67, 148
discipline relaxed, 140
intersection with, 32
negotiation locale, 47, 140, 148
permanent, 56, 139
rapporteurs, 66, 149
reforms, 71–72, 139–40
report, 68
sequence with floor stage, 67
size, 140
subcommittees, 18, 71

Committees, chamber *(continued)*
tasks, 59–64
temporary, 57–58
vote alignments, 67
Communist legislatures, 54, 105
See also Poland; Postcommunist
legislatures
Confidence, vote of no-, 51, 77, 80–81
constructive vote, 81
Conservative Coalition (United
States), 52–53
Constituencies, electorates, 17, 19,
105, 135
Continental (European) models of
parliaments, 11, 12, 42, 43, 49,
138
Czech Republic, 66
Czechoslovakia, 119, 121, 123, 125

DeJouvenel, Bertrand, 28
Democracy and legislature, 1, 10
Denmark, 100, 123, 126
Dole, Robert, senator, 77
Dual-branch system, 7, 36, 74
confirmation of personnel, 92
Congress independent of executive, 7
divided party control, 79–80

Elections
candidate centered, 101, 135
chief executives in legislative
elections, 102
competition, interparty, 105
controversies, 97, 111–14
districting, 106–7, 112
finance of campaigns, 107–8, 113
frequency, 100–101
general, 102–5
incumbents, 103, 105, 106, 107–8
majority vote count rule, 95
Matthew effect, 99
multimember districts, 95, 97, 102,
106
nominations, 101–2
party list ballot, 95
plurality vote count method, 97–98
political action committees (PACs),
107–8

Elections *(continued)*
proportional representation, 95–97,
102
public campaign finance, 107
reforms, 97, 111–14
right to vote, 5, 20, 27, 38, 111–12, 114
selection means, 5
single-member district, 95–96, 102,
106
term (length) of office, 15, 100–101
threshold vote, 38, 96, 99
upper chambers, 112–14
vote
changes, interparty, 103–5
counting methods, 95–96
distortion, 99
wasted, 97
voter turnout, 103
Executive. *See* Chief executive;
Government, cabinet and chief
executive
External factors in policy activity,
132–33, 143
Estonia, 119
Euro-communism, 38
European Common Market, 38, 52, 77

Federalism, 24, 26
Finland, 79, 82
Floor
committees, sequence with, 67
crossing, 39, 41
debate management, 149
schedule, 42, 46, 149
ritualistic, 145
predictable, 145
seating, 39
voting, 50–52, 150
France, 33, 36, 59, 66
assembly and government, 135
cohabitation, 80
committee amendments, 85
constitution, 142
elections, 135
members, 19, 20, 24
French Revolution, 39
Front bench, 43
Fulbright, William, senator, 60–61

Gandhi, Indira, prime minister, 102
George, David Lloyd, 26
Germany
  committees, 57–58, 71–72, 85
  bicameralism, 70, 90
  budget, 61–64, 89–90
  Bundesrat, 26, 89
  chancellor selection, 82–83
  Committee of Elders, 42
  committee system, 57, 59, 67
  constructive vote of no confidence, 81
  documents, 68, 69
  elections, 95, 100–110
  floor, 65
  government, 58–59, 65, 78, 126
  independence from government,
    134, 135
  interest groups, 88, 109, 110
  interest groups and members, 25
  legislation, 84
  legislative stages, 146
  member
    background, 21, 22, 23
    use of time, 17–18
  multiparty system, 35–36
  parliamentary parties, Fraktionen,
    46, 41, 49, 139
  party leader selection, 44
  parties, 25, 37, 38, 81, 83
  Weimar Republic, 33, 81, 96
Gingrich, Newt, U.S. representative, 45
Government, cabinet and chief executive
  ambition, member, 28
  coalition, 81
  constraint on legislature, 134
  legislation preparation, 89, 142
  majority, 79, 138
  minority, 50, 51, 81, 125, 138
  oversized coalition, 81
  relations with legislature
    additional, 89–92
    on legislation, 83–89
    troubled, 92–93
  parliamentary and dual-branch
    systems compared, 74–79
  selection of candidates, 82–83
  stability, 33, 81, 98, 138
Grievances, 4

Hansard Society, 58, 89
Havel, Vaclav, president, 21, 130
Health policy (United States), 47, 110,
  111
Hitler, Adolph, 10
Hungary, 128

Institutionalization, 132–33, 143
  committees, 139–41
  members, 141
  parliamentary parties, 138–39
  resource for action, 137
  schedule, time, 141–42
  staff support, 141
Interest groups, 88, 135
  administrative agencies, 109, 136
  committee, legislative, 109
  conflict, degree of, 136–37
  consulted, 110
  corporatism, 110, 137
  lobbyists, 17
  member affiliations, 24–25
  public campaigns, 110–11, 136
Israel, 27, 83
Italy, 22, 33, 35, 38, 112, 123

Japan, 22, 53, 80–81, 112
Jasinowski, Jerry, 16
Jefferson, Thomas, 120
Johnson, Lyndon, president, 27
Judiciary, 1, 4, 6, 8, 9

Kennedy, John F., president, 76
Kohl, Helmut, chancellor, 102

Lamont, Norman, MP, 48
Latin America, 133
Left–right continuum, 37–38
Legislative procedure, 145
Legislature, as type of institution
  collective decision making, 5
  conflict expression and resolution, 1,
    7–8, 9
  constitutive attributes, 3–6
  contradictions, 1
  democratic legislatures, few, 10
  elective, 5
  equality of members, 4, 7

Legislature, as type of institution
    (continued)
  executive, contrast with, 5, 6, 8
  functions, 6–7
  geographic representation, 4, 27
  internal organization, 7, 31–33,
      54–55, 56–59, 132–33, 143
  law, source of, 2, 6–7
  numerous members, 4,5, 7, 31
  origins, 4
  partisanship, 7,8, 50
  policy, 6, 9–12, 132
  procedures, 7, 42, 121, 145–51
  public accessibility, 1, 8, 49
  public attitudes, 7, 9, 127–28
  public visibility, 8–9
  representation, 4, 6, 8, 17–25
  votes, 5
  See also Chief executive
Legislature, as word, 74
Lenin, V.I., 56, 57
Lobby, lobbyists. *See* Interest groups

Madison, James, 116
Major, John, prime minister, 44, 48,
    52, 77, 78, 80
Members
  activities, 17–18
  changes, 27–28, 141
  constituency work, 17, 19
  demography and politics, 27
  discontent, 28
  education, 21
  equality of, 4, 7
  ethnicity, 23, 25
  experience, prior, 141
  fit with institution, 27–29
  freshmen, 19
  gender, 23
  geographic representation, 27
  government salary, 76
  incumbents, 15
  institutional impact, 15, 16–17, 24,
      27–28, 141
  interest group affiliations, 24
  legislative activity, 19
  legislature-local, holding dual office,
      24

Members *(continued)*
  mirror theory of representation, 27
  newcomers, 13, 27–28
  occupations, 20–21
  office experience, 23–24
  part-time members, 25
  policy advocates, 18
  religion, 23
  representatives, 17–25, 26–27, 29
  roles, 18–20
  social structure, 20–21, 24–25,
      26–27
  changes, 20
  strain on family, 145
  tenure, length, 15–16, 19
  time, use of, 17–18
  turnover, 17
  upper chambers, 25
  virtuous spiral, 29
Michel, Robert, U.S. House
    Republican leader, 45
Mitchell, George, senator, 77
Models of parliaments
  committees, 57–59, 138
  whole systems, 7, 11–12, 132
Monetary policy, 47, 135, 136
Mulroney, Brian, prime minister, 102

Netherlands, 33, 82
Nigeria, 33
Nixon, Richard, president, 52
Norway, 51

Parliament, as word, 74
Parliamentary systems, 36, 74–79,
    133–34
Parties, political
  catch-all, 38–39
  center, 37
  chamber committees, compared
      with, 137–38, 140
  Christian, 37
  cohesion, 50–52
  committees, internal, 32, 47, 66,
  communist
    ruling, 54, 137
    Western Europe, 37–38
  competition, 105

Parties, political *(continued)*
  conservative, 37
  cooperative antagonists, 32, 66
  discipline, 49–50, 67
  elections, parties in, 101–5
  ethnic, 38
  external units, 53–54
  factionalism, 52–53
  floor votes, 50–52
  greens, 38, 95
  ideological spectrum, 37–39
  leaders, 43–6
  leader selection, 83
  liberal, 37
  majority, 43, 89, 138–39, 149
  meetings, 47–49
  minority, 44–45, 138
  negotiate with government, 46, 66,
    72, 138
  negotiation, 42, 66, 138
  nomination control, 101
  opposition, 43, 44, 46, 138
  party-free voting, 49, 51, 52, 67
  party group in legislature, 39–53,
    138–39
  party-loyal voting, 50
  postcommunist, 121
  postindustrial parties, 5
  rebellion, 50
  socialist, 37, 52
  three line whip, 46
  whip, 27, 46
  whip notice, 46
Parties, political; by name
  Bloc Quebecois (Canada), 27, 98
  Christian Democratic Union (CDU;
    Germany), 25, 37, 38
  Christian Democratic (Italy), 37
  Conservative (Britain), 24, 44, 47,
    48, 103
  Communist (France), 38
  Communist (Italy), 38
  Communist (Sweden), 64–65
  Democratic (United States), 52–53,
    55, 99, 107
  Free Democratic (Germany), 38, 81
  Greens (Germany), 38
  Greens (Sweden), 38, 65

Parties, political; by name *(continued)*
  Labour (Britain), 24, 37, 39, 44, 47,
    51, 53–54, 79, 103
  Labour (Israel), 83
  Liberal Democratic (Britain), 53, 97,
    99
  Liberal Democratic (Japan), 53,
    80–81
  Likud (Israel), 83
  Moderate Unity (Sweden), 37
  National Republican Convention
    (Nigeria), 33
  People's (Austria), 37
  People's (Sweden), 37
  Progressive Conservative (Canada),
    83, 105
  Republican (United States), 45,
    52–53, 108
  Social Democratic (Scandinavian),
    36
  Social Democratic (Sweden), 64–65,
    72
  Social Democratic (Nigeria), 33
  Socialist, of Germany (SPD;
    Germany), 25, 81, 83
Party system, 32
  fragmentation, 33, 36
  multiparty, 33, 35–36, 42, 43, 65, 67,
    95, 138, 149
  one-party, 32, 54
  several-party, 36, 138
  two-and-half party, 36
  two-party, 32, 34, 39, 42, 65, 95, 149
Perez, S., 83
Perot, Ross, 107
Petitions, 4
Poland
  elections, 123
  martial law, 128
  Sejm, 67, 70, 91, 124, 125, 126, 127,
    143, 144
  shuttle method, 150
  Solidarity, 121–22, 124, 127
Policy activity by legislatures, factors,
  10, 12, 132–43
Policy attributes, 132–3
  content, 142
  controversiality, 142

Policy attributes *(continued)*
new *vs.* old, 47, 142
stages of policy cycle, 142
visibility, 142
Portugal, 103
Postcommunist legislatures, 38
authoritarian system transformation,
10, 116, 133
bicameralism, 126
central site, 115
chief executive, 126
Communist inheritance, 117, 120,
128–29
Communist rule, collapse of, 118
constitution, 126–27
elections, 10, 122–29
mass media, 128
members, 13, 21, 117–19, 129
multiethnic states, 124
personal conduct, 120–21
political gremium, 119
political parties, 65, 121–24
precedent, lack of, 116
presiding officer, 120–21
presidium, 119
prime minister appointment, 126
public attitudes, 10, 127–28
rules, procedures, 121
staff organization, 125
Power of purse, 6, 89
Public acessibility
attitudes, 7, 9, 128
of committees, 68, 148
of legislative parties, 49, 68, 148
of legislatures, 1, 8–9, 87

Question time, 91

Rabin, Yitzhak, prime minister, 83
Reagan, Ronald, president, 37, 47,
90
Roll call votes, 50–52
Romania, 127
Roosevelt, Franklin, president, 79
Russian Republic, 129–30

Scandinavia, 3, 23, 36, 37, 82
Schedule, 14–15

Separation of powers. *See*
Dual-branch system
Shadow cabinet, 44
Soviet Union, 123, 128–30, 133
Spain, 3, 104
Speaker, the, 41–42, 147
Staff, personnel, 125, 141
Sweden
administrative structure, 135
commissions, prelegislative, 87,
135, 147
committees, 16, 57, 59, 65, 67, 68,
69, 70, 140
documents, 69
election, 96, 99, 100, 103
floor, 67
government, 33, 50, 78
minority, 50
historical continuity, 143
independence of government, 72, 133
interest groups, 110
members, 22, 24
parties, 85, 137, 139
internal structure, 46, 48
motions, 147
negotiations, 59
system, 33, 35
private member, 85
tenure, length, 16
vote by party, 51
Switzerland, 100, 103

Thatcher, Margaret, prime minister,
37, 43–44, 80, 82
Thomas, Clarence, Supreme Court
justice, 92
Tower, John, senator, 92
Turnout, voter, 103

U.S. Congress
administration bill, 86
budget, 89
cabinet, 67
caucus, 48
committee chairs, 65
committees, 56, 57–58, 67, 68, 70,
88, 92, 120, 136, 137, 139, 143,
147, 148, 149

U.S. Congress *(continued)*
confirmation, Senate, 92
congressional parties, 47, 48
conservative coalition, 52–53
constituents, 19
Democratic Study Group, 53
deviant case, Congress as, 134, 143
districts, 106, 112
documents, 69
elections, 27, 135
executive branch, 67
First Congress, 116–17
floor, 50, 149–50
freshmen classes, large, 27–8
gerrymander, 107
government, 76–78, 88
House of Representatives, 34, 41, 45, 57, 149
interest groups, 16, 17, 107–11, 135
key roll calls, 50
legislation, 19, 84
Legislative Reorganization Act, 71
legislative stages, 146
members, 21, 22, 23, 24
party control
   divided, House and Senate, 79
   split, President–Congress, 36
party-free voting, 49, 51–52, 67
party organization, 138

U.S. Congress *(continued)*
political action committees, 107–08
precedents, 116
president, 27–28, 37, 47, 52, 76, 77, 79, 86, 88, 90, 107, 111, 150
president and congressional elections, 79, 102, 105
prelegislative stages, 87–88, 47, 147
primary elections, 101–2
roll call votes, 50
rules, 120
schedule, 149–50
second reading, 146
Senate direct election, 25, 113–14
Southern Democrats, 52–55
subcommittees, 28
tenure, 16–17, 19, 28
two-party system, 65
veto, 150
U.S. model of legislature, 11–12, 134, 143

Walesa, Lech, president, 21, 126, 130
Weimar Republic (Germany), 33, 81, 96
Westminster model of parliaments, 11–12, 39, 43, 51, 57, 67, 91, 148, 149
Wilson, Woodrow, 56, 57

Yeltsin, Boris, president, 10, 129, 130

About the Author

David M. Olson is Professor of Political Science at the University of North Carolina-Greensboro. His research interests include comparative parliaments, the democratization process in Central Europe, and representation in federal systems. His recent books include *Legislatures in the Policy Process: The Dilemmas of Economic Policy* (1991) and *Representation and Policy Formation in Federal Systems: Canada and the United States* (1993).